BORDER COLLIE
Training

Complete Guide to Educating, Training, Communicating with Your Dog, and Understanding Its Language.

Tommaso Cominotti

Table of contents

Introduction:

"If you think dogs can't count, try putting three dog biscuits in your pocket and then give him only two of them."
Phil Pastoret

You've just adopted a Border Collie or you've had this wonderful dog for some time, and you're looking for answers to your most pressing questions. How to educate, train, and socialize your Border Collie? How to decipher his language and communicate effectively with him? If these questions are close to your heart, then you've come to the right place.

Welcome to the exciting world of Border Collie education, a comprehensive guide designed for enthusiastic beginners and dedicated professionals looking to understand and educate this extraordinary breed of dog. This book is much more than just a manual; it is a companion on your journey, a reliable friend who will accompany you at every step of your Border Collie journey.
Imagine yourself walking side by side with your dog, a relationship based on trust, communication, and companionship. Every moment spent together becomes an opportunity for mutual learning, discovery, and strengthening of the unique bond that unites you.

This book doesn't just provide you with dry information and theories; it offers practical, step-by-step guides to implementing the teachings. We have ensured that every piece of information is practical, explained in detail, with concrete examples to guide you.

What to do if your dog refuses to obey a command? We have the answer. How to welcome your Border Collie? We've got it all covered. How to handle undesirable behaviors or prevent common health problems? You'll find the answers in this book.

Border Collie education is an exciting adventure, an exploration of the relationship between humans and dogs, and we are here to guide you every step of the way. Whether you are an enthusiastic novice, an experienced dog owner, or a professional eager to learn more, you will find smart advice, creative tips, and a practical approach to educating your Border Collie in this book.
Prepare to dive into a world where every interaction with your dog becomes a learning opportunity, where every challenge is a chance to grow together, and where every moment spent with your Border Collie is precious.

We are excited to take you on this journey, to share our knowledge and passion for Border Collies, and to help you create a harmonious, fulfilling, and exceptional relationship with your four-legged companion.

So whether you are ready to begin your journey with a new Border Collie puppy or deepen your bond with a long-time companion, this book is for you. Let us be your guide, and together, let's explore the wonders of Border Collie education. Your adventure begins here.

Border Collie: An Exceptional Dog Breed.

The Origin and Evolution of the Dog.

The origin and evolution of the Border Collie dog can be traced back to the hills and pastures of Great Britain. This breed was specially developed for herding work and quickly became a favorite among dog lovers due to its remarkable skills and devotion to its owners. It is known for its attentive personality and high intelligence, making it an exceptional companion for active families and individuals seeking mental stimulation. They are highly adaptable and quick learners, making them ideal for activities such as herding, agility, and, of course, obedience. While the Border Collie has roots in pastoral work, it has also excelled in other roles such as therapy or assisting people with disabilities. It is a dog that thrives on mental and physical challenges, whether you live in an apartment or a house with a garden, as long as it receives sufficient exercise and stimulation.

Many heartwarming stories recount the contributions of Border Collies to improving their owners' lives. For example, there's the story of Max, a Border Collie specially trained to accompany a child with anxiety disorders, helping the child manage their emotions and gain confidence.

In summary, the Border Collie is an exceptional dog breed, valued for its versatile skills, intelligence, and loyalty. If you are a Border Collie owner or considering adopting one, take the time to understand this breed and provide a life rich in activities and challenges in accordance with their needs.

The Different Varieties of Border Collies.

The Border Collie is a dog breed known for its intelligence, agility, and herding abilities. Although there are different lines and types of Border Collies, there are generally no officially recognized varieties by major canine breed organizations such as the Fédération Cynologique Internationale (FCI) or the American Kennel Club (AKC). However, there are subtle differences between Border Collie lines in terms of appearance and behavioral traits.

Here are some of the Border Collie lines and types that are sometimes distinguished by breeders and enthusiasts:

1. **Working Line**: These Border Collies are bred for their herding abilities. They are generally smaller and more agile than show-line Border Collies. They have a strong work ethic, high intelligence, and a great ability to obey commands.
2. **Show Line**: This lineage emphasizes physical appearance more, meaning these Border Collies are generally larger, more muscular, and have denser coats. However, they may not possess the same working instincts as working-line Border Collies.
3. **Border Collies with Varied Coat Colors and Patterns**: Some Border Collie lines have developed by focusing on specific coat colors, such as merle, tricolor, or black and white. However, it is essential to note that priority should always be given to health and skills rather than coat color.
4. **Performance Border Collies**: These dogs are bred to excel in canine sports such as agility, flyball, obedience, and frisbee. They are generally very athletic and have high energy levels.

5. **Companion Border Collies**: While all Border Collies have working abilities and instincts, some are bred more to be family pets and companions. They may have a calmer temperament compared to working-line Border Collies.

Note that regardless of the type of Border Collie, they generally share key characteristics such as intelligence, quick learning ability, and the need for intense mental and physical exercise. If you are considering adopting a Border Collie, make sure to understand the specific needs of the breed and choose a puppy based on your goals and lifestyle.

.

Physical Appearance:

The Border Collie is a breed that places great importance on its physical characteristics, closely linked to its mental and physical abilities. Breed standards define the essential traits to identify a true Border Collie:

- The Border Collie is of medium size, with powerful musculature and an elegant appearance. Its head is well-proportioned to the body, with a slightly rounded skull and a pronounced stop. Its coat is double, consisting of a dense undercoat and longer, more resistant topcoat.
- The physical characteristics of the Border Collie can vary depending on the breeding lines and objectives. For example, dogs intended for competition may have more developed musculature and a more sloping backline than those bred for other tasks.
- The health and well-being of the Border Collie are also important regarding its physical appearance. Poor dental health, overweight, or poorly maintained coat can lead to long-term health problems.
- Breed standards define a range of sizes and weights for the Border Collie, although these figures may vary depending on the breeding lines. On average, the height ranges from 46 to 56 cm for males and from 46 to 53 cm for females. The average weight varies between 14 and 20 kg for males and between 12 and 19 kg for females. However, these values are averages and may vary for each individual.

Here are the average dimensions and weight according to gender:

- For males, the height ranges from 46 to 56 cm with a weight ranging from 14 to 20 kg.
- For females, the height ranges from 46 to 53 cm with a weight ranging from 12 to 19 kg.

The Different Physical Aspects:

1. **Head**: The Border Collie has a head that is proportional to its size, with a slightly rounded skull and a pronounced stop. Its eyes are of medium size, almond-shaped, and dark in color. The ears are erect and well-set.
2. **Body**: Its body is muscular and well-proportioned, with a straight backline, sloping croup, and deep chest. Its limbs are strong and well-muscled, with round feet and thick pads for good grip.
3. **Tail**: Its tail is shaped like a saber, slightly curved downward, and reaches at least to the hock. It is carried slightly upward.
4. **Eyes**: Its eyes are of medium size, almond-shaped, dark in color, and well-spaced. They should express vivacity and intelligence.
5. **Ears**: Its ears are of medium size, erect, and well-set, proportionate to the head, and carried vertically.
6. **Legs**: The Border Collie's legs are muscular and well-proportioned to the body. They are straight and parallel, with round feet and thick pads for good traction.
7. **Musculature**: The Border Collie is muscular and well-proportioned, with developed musculature to support its physical activities. The muscles are firm and well-defined without being prominent.
8. **Silhouette**: Overall, the Border Collie's silhouette should be well-balanced, with harmonious proportions between different parts of the body. Its gait should be light and powerful, demonstrating agility and energy.

In addition to its remarkable appearance, the Border Collie is known for its strength, endurance, loyalty, and intelligence. In summary, the physical aspects of the Border Collie are essential for the breed, as they are linked to its mental and physical capabilities. Established breed standards define the physical characteristics, but it is crucial to consider the health and well-being of the Border Collie in its care. Average dimensions are established based on gender, but each individual may have variations within these size and weight ranges.

Coat Specifics.

The Border Collie's coat is also double, consisting of a dense undercoat and longer, tougher guard hairs. This double layer of fur provides excellent thermal insulation, particularly useful for Border Collies working outdoors in cold weather.

The undercoat is soft and dense, maintaining the dog's body temperature. The guard hair is longer and sturdier than the undercoat, and it is more visible. It protects the undercoat and the dog's skin from external elements such as rain, snow, thorns, insects, etc. The coat can come in various colors, ranging from blue merle, red merle, black tricolor, red tricolor, and more. The Border Collie's coat requires regular maintenance to remain healthy and in good condition. Regular brushing helps remove dead hair, prevent matting, and stimulate blood circulation. Baths should be given sparingly to avoid disrupting the natural balance of the coat and skin.

Coat Colors:

Border Collies come in a variety of colors and distinctive markings, making them not only beautiful but also suited for specific roles based on their characteristics. Here is an exploration of the main types of Border Collies and their utility:

1. **Black and White**: This is the classic type that comes to mind when thinking of Border Collies. These dogs are often used as working dogs for gathering and managing livestock, thanks to their agility, intelligence, and ability to control herd movements.
2. **Black Tricolor**: This variant adds red markings to the black and white coat. Black tricolor Border Collies generally share the same abilities as black and white ones, but their red markings can make them even more visible and easy to spot in the field.
3. **Blue and White**: Blue and white Border Collies are a diluted version of the black and white ones. They are also used in herding work and can be equally effective, although their appearance is slightly different.

4. **Blue Merle**: These Border Collies have mainly white/grayish fur with black/blue patches. Their striking appearance often makes them popular show dogs, but their intelligence and energy make them excellent candidates for various activities, such as agility and canine sports.
5. **Slate Merle**: Similar to blue merle but in a diluted version. These dogs can have similar characteristics to blue merles but with softer nuances.
6. **Blue Tricolor**: The base color is blue merle, punctuated with fire-colored markings. They share similarities with blue merles in terms of utility, with the addition of fire markings.
7. **Chocolate and White**: Although unofficial, this variant is common. Chocolate and white Border Collies have mainly brown fur speckled with white. Their active temperament and ability to learn make them excellent for various agility and canine sports activities.
8. **Chocolate Tricolor**: This variant adds fire markings to the chocolate and white coat, which can make them even more spectacular in the field.
9. **Lilac and White**: Similar to chocolate and white but in a diluted version, these dogs can be used similarly to chocolate and white, although their coat may be a bit less common.
10. **Red and White**: Liver color replaces black, creating a red and white coat. Although less common, this variant can also be used for herding work.
11. **Sable and White**: A rare color that replaces black with sand in the black and white coat. Although uncommon, these dogs can have similar qualities to black and white ones.

Each variety of Border Collie has unique characteristics, but most share exceptional intelligence, high energy, and a strong work ethic, making them incredible partners for a variety of roles and activities, whether it's working with herds, participating in canine sports, or becoming loving and active family companions.

In general, the Border Collie's coat is dense, thick, and shiny, with longer fur around the neck, shoulders, legs, and tail. The undercoat is also dense and soft, helping to insulate the dog against cold temperatures. The color of the coat can vary depending on age, genetics, and environment.

Its Silhouette and Measurements.

The Border Collie is a medium-sized dog with an athletic and elegant appearance. It has a well-proportioned head, a strong muzzle, and upright ears. Its body is muscular and well-proportioned, with strong legs and robust claws. Its tail is naturally long and straight, reaching the level of its hocks. It has a dense double-layer coat that is weather-resistant, with stiff and shiny hair. Its coat comes in a variety of colors, including blue merle, red merle, black tricolor, and red tricolor. The different stages of physical development and maturity of the Border Collie, from a young age:

- **At 2 months,** the Border Collie is an adorable little puppy with soft fur and a curious look at the world.
- **At 6 months,** it begins to develop its musculature, and its fur becomes denser and more resistant.
- **From 1 year onwards,** the Border Collie is considered a mature adult, displaying a well-defined silhouette and developed musculature.
- **At the age of 7,** it may be considered an older dog but still retains its distinctive beauty and charming presence.
- **Adult Size:** The Border Collie usually reaches its adult size between 18 and 24 months of age.

It is worth noting that the physical development and maturity of a Border Collie depend on various factors, including its diet, level of exercise, overall health, and genetic heritage. Regular maintenance is also essential to preserve the beauty and health of its coat, as well as to ensure its longevity and well-being.

Its price:

The cost of a Border Collie can vary depending on several factors, such as geographical location, pedigree, age, gender, and physical characteristics. In general, Border Collies are considered a valuable dog breed due to their intelligence, hard work, and charm.

1. **In France,** the average price of a Border Collie puppy from a reputable breeder generally ranges between 800 and 2000 euros, depending on the puppy's characteristics and the quality of the breeding. Adult dogs can be more expensive, especially if they have been trained for specific tasks such as herding, canine sports, or assistance.
2. **In other parts of the world,** the cost of a Border Collie also varies depending on various factors. In the United States, the average price of a Border Collie puppy ranges between 800 and 1500 US dollars, while in the United Kingdom, it can vary between 500 and 2000 British pounds. In countries like Australia and Canada, prices can be similar.

The high demand for Border Collies is attributed to their agility, dedication, versatility, and ability to excel in a variety of fields. They are also known for their athletic silhouette and elegant coat. However, it is important to note that Border Collies can have hereditary health problems, such as hip dysplasia, leading to additional healthcare costs for owners.

Due to the popularity of Border Collies, it is essential to exercise caution when purchasing a puppy of this breed. It is recommended to turn to trusted breeders who provide information about the pedigree, health status, and behavior of the puppies. Prospective owners should also avoid irresponsible breeding practices, such as puppy mills, which can harm the health and well-being of dogs.

Personality and Behavior:

The Border Collie, famous for its intelligence, agility, and passion for work, is a dog breed that garners the admiration and interest of many dog owners. This chapter delves deeply into the personality and complex behavior of this extraordinary breed. By better understanding the distinctive traits of Border Collies, you will be better prepared to meet their needs and cultivate a harmonious relationship with them.

- ✔ **Exceptional Intelligence and Mental Abilities:** Border Collies are widely regarded as one of the most intelligent dog breeds. Their quick learning ability, problem-solving skills, and aptitude for understanding human cues make them exceptional working and companion partners. Their high intelligence demands constant mental stimulation to prevent boredom, which can lead to undesirable behaviors such as property destruction.
- ✔ **Urgent Need for Work and Activity:** The Border Collie's personality is deeply rooted in its fervent desire to work. Originally bred to gather and control herds of sheep, these dogs possess endless energy and unwavering focus when engaged in a task. An inactive Border Collie can develop destructive or anxious behaviors. Therefore, it is essential to provide this breed with mentally and physically stimulating activities.
- ✔ **Sensitivity to Social Cues:** Border Collies have a remarkable ability to read and respond to social cues. They can subtly detect human emotions, making them sensitive to their owner's mood. This ability can strengthen the bond between the dog and its owner but can also lead to high levels of anxiety if the dog perceives stress or agitation in its owner.
- ✔ **Tendency to Overexert:** The enthusiasm and perseverance of Border Collies can sometimes lead them to overexertion. They can become deeply engrossed in a task to the point of ignoring their own fatigue or signs of physical distress. Owners must closely monitor their dog's limits to prevent injuries or exhaustion.
- ✔ **Trainability and Need for Consistency:** Border Collies excel in training due to their intelligence and desire to please their owners. However, their sharp minds can also make them stubborn if they perceive inconsistencies in expectations or rewards. Positive and consistent training is essential to channel their energy and promote desirable behaviors.
- ✔ **Gathering and Control Instincts:** The gathering instinct is deeply rooted in the genes of Border Collies. Even in the absence of herds, some individuals may exhibit this behavior by trying to gather objects or even other animals. Early socialization and appropriate redirection of these instincts are crucial to prevent these behaviors from becoming problematic.
- ✔ **Strong Attachment:** Border Collies are known for their deep attachment to their owners. They often seek human company and can develop close bonds with their family. This attachment can sometimes make them dependent, highlighting the importance of maintaining a balance between independence and social interaction.

In terms of personality, Border Collies are intelligent, loyal, active and hard-working dogs. They are often used in herding roles and are renowned for their dedication and problem-solving skills. They are also protective and affectionate towards their families, making them an excellent choice of companion for those looking for a loyal dog. However, it's important to note that Border Collies can be wary of strangers. Early and continuous socialization is crucial to avoid undesirable behavior.

In terms of health, the Border Collie may be predisposed to certain hereditary conditions such as hip dysplasia, eye problems, etc. Regular health examinations with the veterinarian are essential to detect and treat health problems as soon as they arise.

In conclusion, the Border Collie is a versatile and devoted dog suitable for various roles and situations. With regular maintenance and proper socialization, it can be the ideal companion for active and committed owners looking for an intelligent, protective, and loyal dog.

Its Behavior Within the Family?

The Border Collie is an extremely loyal dog to its family and owners. It has a strong desire to please its master and often develops deep bonds with them. It can be an excellent, calm, and relaxed companion, but it can also be playful and lively when stimulated. Proper training and socialization are recommended to prevent any aggressive or anxious behavior. In general, the Border Collie is protective and vigilant, loving to be close to its family and loved ones.

The Border Collie is also a accomplished working dog, always in search of purpose and tasks to accomplish. It can be trained for various tasks, including obedience, protection, search, and rescue. It is essential to note that this breed of dog needs exercise and attention to be happy and balanced. If you are considering adopting a Border Collie, be sure to devote enough quality time and exercise to meet its needs.

Its Behavior with Children?

Just like with adults, a Border Collie's behavior towards children depends on various factors, such as early socialization, training, and previous experiences. In general, the Border Collie is intelligent, loyal, and protective, making it an excellent companion for children if well-trained and socialized. However, it is important to monitor interactions between children and the dog to prevent any incidents. Children should also learn to respect boundaries and safety rules to ensure the safety of the dog and themselves.

It is crucial to note that some Border Collies may exhibit behavioral issues, such as aggression, which can be caused by factors like neglect, abuse, or excessive overprotection. Therefore, it is paramount to acquire a puppy from a reputable breeder and properly socialize and educate the dog from a young age to minimize the risk of undesirable behaviors.

Overall, the Border Collie can be an excellent companion for children if properly trained and socialized. However, due to its size and strength, it is crucial to supervise interactions between children and the dog to avoid any issues. Here are some details and examples of its behavior with children:

1. It is a protective and loyal dog, capable of developing close bonds with the family. It can be an excellent companion for children and protect them if necessary.
2. It is an intelligent and easy-to-train dog, making it an excellent companion for children. It can quickly learn to obey simple commands and respect the boundaries set by the owners.
3. It requires exercise and mental stimulation to be happy and balanced. It can be an excellent playmate for children and help them channel their energy in a positive way.
4. Children must also learn to respect boundaries and safety rules to avoid putting the dog or themselves in danger.

It is important to teach children these basic safety rules when interacting with dogs. Here are some examples:

1.	Always ask the owner's permission before touching the dog.
2.	Do not disturb the dog while it is eating or sleeping.
3.	Do not pull the dog's ears, tail, or fur.
4.	Do not run or shout around the dog; it can stress and make the dog anxious.
5.	Do not leave young children alone with the dog without adult supervision.
6.	Learn to read the dog's body language signs, such as signs of stress or threat, to know when the dog is not comfortable.
7.	Avoid rough play or aggressive behavior with the dog.

By teaching these basic safety rules to children, they can learn to interact appropriately with dogs and avoid putting the dog or themselves in danger. It is also crucial to supervise all interactions between children and the dog to ensure that everything goes smoothly.

In summary, the Border Collie can be an excellent companion for children if properly trained and socialized. However, it is important to give them enough attention and quality time, provide them with proper training, and monitor interactions between children and the dog to prevent any incidents.

Attention: While the Border Collie is generally a gentle and affectionate dog towards children, it can rarely exhibit aggressive or concerning behaviors under the influence of stress and anxiety. If this happens, it is crucial to take immediate steps to ensure the safety of everyone and consult a professional for help and guidance in managing this behavior. It is also important to monitor interactions between children and the dog and teach them to respect boundaries and safety rules. In general, the Border Collie is an ideal dog breed for families with children, but you must remain vigilant and take necessary measures to ensure everyone's safety.

What to Do in Case of Aggression?

Here are some tips on how to behave in case of aggression from your dog:

1. **Stay calm.** Dogs are very sensitive to their owner's emotions, and if you panic or shout, it could worsen the situation.
2. **Move away from them slowly.** If your dog shows signs of aggression or stress, try to move away from them slowly without losing sight of them. Don't turn your back or run, as it can further stimulate them.
3. **If you can't calm them down.** If you feel in danger, don't hesitate to seek help from a third party or call emergency services. Do not try to restrain your dog alone if you do not feel capable of doing so safely.
4. **Make sure the children are immediately safe:** If the dog is still present, place the children in a safe location out of its reach. If necessary, call an ambulance or emergency services for immediate medical attention.
5. **Contact a veterinarian or canine behaviorist:** If you are the dog's owner, immediately contact a veterinarian or canine behaviorist for assistance and advice on managing this behavior. They can assess the dog and help you determine the appropriate measures to take.
6. **Report the incident:** If the dog belongs to someone else, you must report the incident to local authorities, such as the police or animal services. They can assist you in taking appropriate measures to ensure the safety of all children involved.
7. **Avoid blaming the children:** Do not blame the children for the incident, even if you believe they provoked the dog. Children may not understand how their behavior affects a dog or may be too young to comprehend the consequences of their actions.

8. **Avoid punishing the dog:** Avoid punishing the dog for its aggressive behavior. Punishment can worsen the dog's behavior and escalate the situation. Furthermore, it could exacerbate the children's injuries.
9. **Educate children about safety rules with dogs:** It is important to educate children about safety rules with dogs to prevent future incidents. Children need to understand that dogs need space and time for themselves and should never tease or provoke a dog.
10. **Exercise caution with the dog in the future:** If you are the dog's owner, it is important to exercise caution in the future to avoid future incidents. This may include measures such as training your dog, installing fences or safety gates, and closely supervising interactions between the dog and children.

It is essential to take measures to prevent aggression situations with your dog. Ensure to socialize it from a young age and provide proper training to learn how to interact correctly with other dogs and humans. If your dog shows signs of aggression or stress, consult a veterinarian or a behaviorist for assistance.

His behavior with strangers?

The Border Collie is generally a very friendly and sociable dog with strangers, but as with any dog, proper socialization and training are essential to prevent undesirable behavior. It's important to teach your dog from a young age to be comfortable in the presence of strangers and to react appropriately.

Here are some tips for the first encounter between your Border Collie and a stranger to avoid any inappropriate behavior:

1. Inform the stranger to ask for your permission before petting or approaching your dog. Even if it appears friendly, it's important to respect its personal space and have the stranger ask for permission before touching it.
2. Make sure your dog is on a leash or in a secure area to prevent it from running away or rushing towards the stranger. If your dog is off-leash, ensure it is under complete control.
3. Let your dog approach the stranger at its own pace. Don't force it to sniff or be petted by the stranger if it's uncomfortable. Allow it to approach the stranger on its terms and respect its boundaries.
4. Ask the stranger not to make direct eye contact with your dog. Dogs can perceive this as a threat and may react aggressively. Request the stranger to look at your dog from the side or down to show that they are not a threat.
5. Ask the stranger not to touch your dog's head or neck. These areas are considered very sensitive for dogs and can trigger an aggressive reaction if touched abruptly or unwantedly.
6. Avoid stressful or intimidating situations for your dog, such as crowds or loud noises, which can trigger an aggressive reaction.
7. Provide your dog with proper training to handle interactions with strangers. Well-trained dogs are more comfortable and predictable in social situations.

In general, the Border Collie is a very sociable and friendly dog with strangers, but it's important to provide them with good socialization and education to encourage these qualities. By following these simple tips during the initial meeting between your dog and a stranger, you can help ensure that the interaction goes positively and pleasantly for everyone involved.

How Does It Behave with Other Dogs

Regarding the behavior of the Border Collie with other dogs, it generally has a friendly and playful attitude. However, it's essential to consider that each dog has its own personality, and early and appropriate socialization is crucial to foster good interactions. Here are some tips to facilitate meetings between your Border Collie and other dogs:

1. **Early Socialization:** Expose your puppy to well-behaved dogs and social environments from a young age to learn how to interact positively.
2. **Supervision:** Be vigilant during encounters with other dogs, especially in the beginning. Observe signs of play, excitement, and mutual acceptance.
3. **Respect Boundaries:** Ensure your dog respects the communication signals of other dogs and teach them to react appropriately.
4. **Ongoing Training:** Continue to train your Border Collie to maintain good behavioral skills, especially during interactions with other dogs.
5. **Avoiding Conflicts:** Avoid situations where your dog might feel threatened or intimidated by other dogs, as this can trigger aggressive behaviors.

By following these tips and closely monitoring interactions between your Border Collie and other dogs, you can encourage positive and favorable encounters.

How to Separate Dogs in Case of a Fight:

Separating dogs in case of a fight can be a stressful and potentially dangerous situation for owners and the dogs involved. Knowing how to act correctly is essential to minimize the risk of injuries. Here is a practical guide on how to separate your dog from other dogs in case of a fight:

1. **Stay Calm:** Dogs can easily sense fear and stress in their owner, which can escalate the situation. Stay calm and relaxed to help soothe your dog.
2. **Use an Object to Separate the Dogs:** Use an object such as a stick or a chair to separate the dogs to avoid getting bitten or scratched. Avoid using your hands to separate the dogs, as it could injure you.
3. **Avoid Shouting or Panicking:** Shouting or panicking can worsen the situation and make the dogs more aggressive. Speak in a calm and firm voice to try to calm the dogs. To speak in a calm and firm voice, you can use a low and steady tone of voice, without being too loud or too soft. Try to speak determinedly but without being threatening. For example, you can say "Stop" or "Leave" in a firm voice, but without raising your tone. If your dog tends to respond to commands through body language, you can also use a hand gesture to stop or recall them. The important thing is to stay calm and not worsen the situation by shouting or panicking.
4. **Use Treats:** If dogs are fighting over a resource, such as food or a toy, use treats to distract your dog and remove them from the situation.
5. **Use an Anti-Aggression Spray:** If your dog is frequently involved in fights with other dogs, you can use an anti-aggression spray specially designed for dogs to calm your dog and prevent a dangerous situation.
6. **Consider Consulting a Professional:** If your dog is frequently involved in fights with other dogs, it's important to consult a professional to determine the underlying cause of aggressive behavior and get advice on managing this situation.

It is crucial to understand that separating dogs in the event of a fight can be a stressful and potentially dangerous situation for all dogs involved. Therefore, it is important to take measures to prevent these situations by closely monitoring interactions between dogs and avoiding areas with a high density of dogs if your dog tends to be aggressive towards other dogs.

What to Do If My Dog Attacks Other Dogs:

If your dog exhibits aggressive behaviors towards other dogs, it is important to take immediate steps to ensure the safety of all dogs involved and to correct your dog's behavior. Here are some safety measures to take in the event of aggressive behavior from your dog towards other dogs:

1. **Put Your Dog on a Leash:** If your dog displays aggressive behavior towards other dogs, it's essential to keep them on a leash to prevent any incidents. If you're in a dog park, keep your dog away from other dogs or leave the park if necessary.

2. **Pay Attention to Body Language:** Body language cues such as growling, raised fur, and a fixed gaze can indicate that your dog is about to exhibit aggressive behavior towards other dogs. Be attentive to these signals and act promptly to prevent any incidents.

3. **Avoid Stressful Situations:** Avoid putting your dog in stressful situations that could trigger aggressive behavior. Stay away from crowded areas and zones with many other dogs.

4. **Consult a Professional:** If your dog displays aggressive behavior towards other dogs, it's important to consult a canine behaviorist or a behavioral veterinarian to help you correct this behavior. They can assist you in understanding the underlying reasons for your dog's aggressive behavior and provide advice on how to correct it.

5. **Avoid Punishing Your Dog:** Avoid punishing your dog for their aggressive behavior towards other dogs. Punishment can worsen your dog's aggressive behavior and make the situation even more dangerous.

6. **Train Your Dog:** Educate your dog using positive reinforcement techniques to reward appropriate behaviors towards other dogs. By reinforcing appropriate behaviors, you can help your dog learn to interact appropriately with other dogs.

In summary, if your dog displays aggressive behaviors towards other dogs, it's important to take immediate steps to ensure the safety of all the dogs involved. Avoid stressful situations, keep your dog on a leash, and be attentive to your dog's body language. Consult a canine behaviorist or a behavioral veterinarian to help correct this behavior, and educate your dog using positive reinforcement techniques to reward appropriate behaviors towards other dogs.

In summary, if your Border Collie displays aggressive behaviors towards other dogs, it is crucial to take immediate measures to ensure the safety of all dogs involved. Avoid stressful situations, keep your dog on a leash, be attentive to body signals, and consult a professional for advice and solutions to correct this behavior. With the right approach, your Border Collie can learn to interact positively with other dogs.

How to Manage Undesirable Behaviors?

Here's how to handle different situations if your dog is shy, wary, or aggressive towards other dogs:

What to do if your dog is shy and wary?

1. Start with gentle and safe socialization sessions, such as walks in parks with few people and dogs.
2. If your dog is shy with other dogs, it's essential to socialize them properly from a young age to help them overcome their shyness. You can take them for walks in places with other dogs and let them interact under your supervision, ensuring they are not too stressed.

3. If your pet is wary of other dogs, give them time to sniff and observe before allowing interaction. You can also use rewards to reinforce positive behavior and ease tensions.

4. If he is aggressive towards other dogs, it is recommended to train him and teach him to control his aggressive instincts. You can work with a professional trainer or follow a training program to help your dog learn to control his aggression. It is also important to monitor interactions between your dog and other dogs and separate them if necessary.

How to train my dog to control his aggression:

Here is a practical guide to help train an aggressive dog towards other dogs:

1. Understanding the Causes of Aggression:

First and foremost, it is crucial to understand the reasons why your dog is aggressive towards other dogs. Is it out of fear, territoriality, or poor socialization? Understanding the cause of their aggression is essential to choose the right training method. Here are some avenues to explore depending on the possible cause of your dog's aggression:

If Your Dog is Fearful:

- Avoid confronting your dog with its fears and forcing it to interact with other dogs.
- Avoid punishing or shouting at your dog for its aggressive behavior, as it will only worsen its fear.
- Use desensitization and counter-conditioning to help your dog associate frightening situations with positive things like treats or play.
- **Desensitization** involves gradually exposing the dog to stimuli that trigger its fear or undesirable behavior while keeping it in a state of calm and relaxation. The idea is to gradually expose the dog to these stimuli so that the dog gradually becomes accustomed to their presence and eventually no longer perceives them as threatening.
- **Counter-Conditioning** involves associating a negative stimulus with a positive stimulus to change the dog's emotional response to that stimulus. For example, if a dog is afraid of children, counter-conditioning involves exposing the dog to children and rewarding it every time it interacts positively with them. The dog then learns to associate the presence of children with something positive rather than negative.

If your dog is territorial:

- If your dog is territorial, it's important to avoid leaving him unsupervised in areas where he might feel threatened, such as the garden, a balcony, or a yard where he can see or hear strangers or other animals passing by. It's also important not to leave your dog alone with unfamiliar visitors in your home and not to leave him alone in a parked car, as this can trigger aggressive behavior. Make sure to introduce your dog appropriately to guests and monitor their interaction to prevent any aggressive behavior.
- Establish clear boundaries for your dog and teach him to respect these boundaries. you can designate a specific space in your home, use a leash or barrier to define areas where your dog can move, teach your dog to stay in a specific place when opening the door, use a crate or kennel to provide a safe and comfortable space for your dog, and use basic commands to teach your dog to respect people and animals in the house. Rewarding good behavior and correcting bad behavior will establish clear and consistent boundaries for your dog.
- Use positive reinforcement techniques to teach your dog to accept other dogs in its territory.

If your dog has been poorly socialized:

- Seek professional help to assist in socializing your dog.
- Start with positive and short interactions with other dogs, gradually increasing the duration and complexity of these interactions.
- Be patient and persistent as socialization can take time and requires patience and consistency.

It's important to note that each case is unique and the causes of your dog's aggression can be multiple and complex. If you have any doubts or questions about managing your dog's aggressive behavior, don't hesitate to consult a professional for personalized help and advice.

2. Avoid risky situations:

To begin with, it is necessary to avoid risky situations where your dog could encounter other dogs. This may include places like dog parks or busy streets. Avoiding these risky situations will help minimize the chances that your dog has a bad experience.

3. Use a muzzle:

If you cannot avoid risky situations, you can use a muzzle to prevent your dog from biting or injuring other dogs. Make sure the muzzle is properly fitted, and your dog can breathe easily.

4. Socialization:

Socializing your dog involves teaching them to interact with people, other dogs, and environments in a positive and safe manner. Start socializing your dog from a young age to maximize their chances of becoming a well-balanced and safe dog in all situations.

Here are some tips for socializing your dog:

1. Introduce your puppy to different people, including men, women, children, seniors, and people with accessories such as hats, glasses, and umbrellas.
2. Introduce your puppy to different types of animals, such as cats and birds, as well as other dogs.
3. Expose your puppy to different types of environments, including cities, parks, beaches, and indoor spaces.
4. Expose your puppy to different types of stimuli, such as traffic sounds, household appliance noises, and car vibrations.
5. Reward your puppy for positive behaviors during socialization and avoid reprimanding or punishing them for undesirable behaviors.

By properly socializing your dog, you can ensure that they will be comfortable and well-balanced in all situations and with all the people and animals they encounter. If you have any questions or concerns about your dog's socialization, consult a professional for advice and assistance.

5. Obedience Training:

Obedience training can help strengthen the bond between you and your dog, as well as teach them to control their aggressive instincts. Obedience training may include basic commands such as "sit,"down," and "stay." Train them in a quiet, distraction-free environment to start, and gradually increase the difficulty.

6. Training with Toys:

Training with toys can help distract your dog when they are confronted with other dogs. Use toys that are durable and easy to clean to avoid choking hazards or infections. Interactive toys can be an excellent way to keep your dog busy and help them focus on something other than their aggression.

7. Positive Reinforcement:

8. Positive reinforcement is important to help your dog learn new behaviors. This can include treats or praise for appropriate behaviors, and ignoring or redirecting for inappropriate behaviors. Avoid physical punishment or yelling as it can worsen the situation.

9. Consult a Professional:

If you are experiencing difficulties with the training of your aggressive dog, do not hesitate to consult a professional for help and advice. A canine behaviorist can assist you in understanding the reasons for your dog's aggression and in developing an appropriate training plan.

What to Do If Your Dog Is Aggressive?

Aggression in dogs can be caused by various factors, including pain, fear, territorial or family protection, play, hunting instinct, and frustration. To understand why your dog is aggressive, it is recommended to pay close attention to your dog's behaviors in order to better understand the causes of its aggression and how to manage this behavior.

Note: To learn what to do in this case, I invite you to read the chapter **"What to Do in the Face of Your Dog's Aggression"**, where I explain step by step what you should do for each situation.

Here are some signs that may indicate the cause of your dog's aggression:

- **Pain:** If he becomes aggressive when touched or handled in certain parts of his body, he may be experiencing pain. In this case, it is crucial to consult a veterinarian to assess the cause of the pain and establish an appropriate treatment plan.
- **Fear:** If he becomes aggressive when confronted with stressful or frightening situations, he may be reacting in this way to protect himself.
- **Territorial or Family Protection:** If he becomes aggressive when confronted by strangers or other animals, he may be reacting in this way to protect his territory or family.
- **Playfulness:** If he becomes aggressive during play, he may have difficulty distinguishing play from reality.
  • Hunting Instinct: If he becomes aggressive when confronted with other animals, it may be due to his hunting instinct.
- **Frustration:** If he becomes aggressive when he cannot access resources or when he is unable to do something he desires, it may be due to frustration.

It's important to remember that these causes of aggression are not exhaustive, and there may be other factors contributing to this behavior in your dog. If you notice signs of aggression in your dog, it's important to consult a professional for assistance in understanding the underlying cause of this behavior.

The Negative Aspects of His Personality.

Just like other dog breeds, the Border Collie has its own personality and may have some flaws. Here are some negative traits of its personality that may require special attention:

1. **High Energy:** The Border Collie is naturally very energetic and requires regular exercise and mental stimulation to stay balanced. If it doesn't expend enough energy, it can become restless or engage in destructive behaviors.
2. **Separation Anxiety:** This dog is usually very attached to its owners and can experience anxiety when left alone for long periods. This can lead to undesirable behaviors such as excessive barking or destruction. Gradually acclimating it to being alone and providing toys and mental activities can help keep it entertained in your absence.
3. **Tendency to Overprotect:** The Border Collie may have a strong protective instinct towards its owners or territory. It's essential to teach it to control this instinct to avoid aggressive reactions in certain situations.

4. **Need for Ongoing Training:** This dog is highly intelligent and requires mental stimulation. Regular and consistent training is necessary to prevent it from becoming stubborn or difficult to handle.
5. **Sensitivity:** The Border Collie can be sensitive to certain situations, such as loud noises or changes in its environment. Early socialization and gradual exposure to different stimuli can help it better manage its emotions.
6. **Tendency to Bark:** It may bark frequently, which can be annoying to those around you. By teaching it to control its barking and providing enough mental stimulation, you can help reduce this behavior.
7. **Grooming Requirements:** Its dense coat requires regular grooming to prevent matting and skin problems. If you can't provide proper grooming, it can lead to health issues.
8. **Predisposition to Certain Health Issues:** Like all dog breeds, the Border Collie can be prone to certain health conditions such as allergies, eye problems, or joint issues. Regular veterinary visits are important to monitor its health and take preventive measures if necessary.

Remember that every dog is unique, and with the right training, socialization, and care, these negative traits can be effectively managed to allow your Border Collie to lead a happy and balanced life.

How to Handle Other Undesirable Behaviors?

Here are some examples of undesirable dog behaviors and what you can do to address them:

If it barks excessively. Here's how to deal with this behavior:

1. **Identify the cause of barking:** It's crucial to determine why your dog is barking in order to find a solution. Is it barking to get your attention? Is it barking because it's scared or anxious? Is it barking out of boredom? Once you've identified the cause of the barking, you can find a solution that suits your dog.
2. **Use rewards to reinforce positive behavior:** You can use rewards, such as treats or praise, to reinforce your dog's positive behavior and encourage it not to bark.
3. **Teach your dog to obey the "no" command:** Teach your dog to obey the "no" command and use it every time it barks inappropriately.
4. **Ensure your dog gets enough exercise and mental stimulation:** If it's bored, it can become restless and bark inappropriately. Ensure that it gets enough exercise and mental stimulation to help it burn off energy and calm down. Here are some mental stimulation exercises:
   - **Walking:** Walking is an excellent exercise to help your dog burn off energy and calm down. You can walk with your dog in a park or a quiet neighborhood to provide exercise and mental stimulation.
   - **Tracking games:** Tracking games involve following a scent trail with your dog. This can be an excellent way to stimulate its mind and help it calm down.
   - **Treasure hunt games:** You can hide treats in your house or garden and let your dog search for them.
   - **Agility games:** Agility games involve guiding your dog through a series of obstacles, such as tunnels, beams, and bars.
   - **Puzzle games:** You can purchase or make toys that challenge your dog's mind and help it solve puzzles. For example, you can use a puzzle to hide food and let your dog figure out how to get it. You can also use toys that require your dog to push or pull to access food.

   These types of games can be an excellent way to stimulate its mind and help it calm down.

If he exhibits other undesirable behaviors:

1. **Ignore the undesirable behavior:** If he exhibits undesirable behavior to get your attention, such as chewing on anything he finds, you can try ignoring him until he calms down. This means not reacting to his behavior by giving him attention, food, or a toy. If he realizes that this behavior doesn't get him what he wants, he may stop doing it. However, it's important not to completely ignore your dog and to provide appropriate attention and affection.

Here are some tips for managing your dog's undesirable behaviors:

- ✔ **Identify the cause of the behavior:** Before you can manage undesirable behavior, you need to understand why your dog is acting this way. Does he need more exercise or mental stimulation? Is he reacting to specific stress or anxiety? Is he trying to communicate something specific? By identifying the cause of the behavior, you can better understand how to manage it appropriately.
- ✔ **Use Positive Training Methods:** To manage your dog's undesirable behaviors, it's important to use positive training methods, which involve rewarding good behavior and ignoring undesirable behavior. You can use treats, praise, or words of approval to reward him when he behaves well and ignore or redirect his attention when he acts undesirably.

- ✔ **Provide Plenty of Exercise and Mental Stimulation:** Your dog needs plenty of exercise and mental stimulation to stay happy and healthy. If you can't provide him with enough intellectual challenges and new experiences, he may become destructive or restless. To help him manage mood swings and excessive barking, you can offer him daily walks, physical games, and activities, as well as interactive toys and mental training exercises.
- ✔ **Take the Time to Educate Him:** Education is essential to help your dog learn the rules of your home and behave appropriately. Take the time to teach him basic commands, such as "sit,"lie down," and "stay," and show him how to behave in society. You can also teach him to respect the boundaries of his territory and not jump on people or bite them.
- ✔ **Take Care of Your Dog:** Your dog needs quality care to be healthy and happy. Make sure to provide him with a balanced diet and the necessary grooming and healthcare. If he is stressed or anxious, you can also offer him relaxation methods, such as soothing music or massages, to help him relax.
- ✔ **Be Consistent in Your Training:** You must be consistent in your training and not give in to your dog's whims. If you allow your dog to do something once, he will try to do it every time he can. By being consistent in your training, you show him what is acceptable and what is not.
- ✔ **Be Patient and Persistent:** Patience and persistence are essential qualities for successful dog training and education. Behavior changes do not happen overnight; it takes time and patience for your dog to assimilate new rules and habits. Be patient with your dog, reward him when he does things correctly, and do not be discouraged by any setbacks. Stay persistent in your efforts to help your dog become a happy and well-balanced companion.

You can apply the same steps to address other undesirable behaviors in your dog:
- **Jumps on People:** If he jumps on people when excited, you can teach him to obey the "sit" command and wait for permission to greet people. You can also teach him to obey the "heel" command to prevent him from jumping on people.
- **Chews on Everything:** If he tends to chew on everything he finds, you can teach him to obey the "leave it" command and not touch objects that are not intended for him. You can also provide him with toys and chew bones to give him an appropriate activity.
- **Barks on Leash:** If he barks on the leash when he sees other dogs or strangers, you can teach him to obey the "enough" command to let him know that this barking is not acceptable. You can also reward him with treats and praise when he remains calm on the leash to reinforce this behavior.

In summary, to manage your dog's undesirable behaviors, you need to understand the cause of the behavior, use positive training methods, provide him with enough exercise and mental stimulation, take the time to educate him, take care of him, be consistent in your training, be patient and persistent, be attentive to his behavior, and consult a professional if necessary.

Adopting a Border Collie.

Adopting a pet is an important decision that requires careful consideration, especially if you are thinking of adopting a Border Collie. Here are some steps to ensure that you make the best choice for both you and your new companion:

- **Reflect on your motivations and lifestyle:** Before deciding to adopt a Border Collie, take the time to reflect on your motivations and lifestyle. Border Collies are intelligent, active, and high-energy dogs that require constant attention and commitment. Make sure your lifestyle can meet their needs in terms of time and interaction.
- **Get to know the breed:** Learn about the specific characteristics, needs, and typical behaviors of the Border Collie. Understand what it entails to welcome this dog into your life and if you're ready to provide what it needs.
- **Find a reputable breeder or shelter:** Look for a reputable breeder or a trusted shelter to adopt your Border Collie. Conduct thorough research, visit the facilities, and ensure that the dogs are well-treated and in good health.
- **Check the animal's health status:** Ensure that the puppy has received necessary vaccinations and care. If you're adopting an adult, request health and vaccination certificates. Also, check that the animal is in good shape and shows no signs of illness.
- **Try cohabitation:** Before making the final decision to adopt a Border Collie, it's recommended to try cohabitation. This will allow you to see how the dog adapts to your home and lifestyle. If you're adopting a Border Collie from a shelter, you can often take the dog to your home for a few days before making your final decision.
- **Prepare your home and yard:** Before the arrival of your Border Collie, ensure that your home is safe for them. Remove anything that could be dangerous for the dog, and make sure your yard is well-fenced and secure.
- **Seek advice from a veterinarian or dog trainer:** Consult a professional for guidance on caring, training, and dealing with the behavior of a Border Collie. They can assist you in addressing any potential issues that may arise.
- **Budget for adoption:** Don't forget to budget for the expenses associated with adopting a dog. Adopting a dog involves anticipated costs such as veterinary fees, food expenses, and maintenance costs. You should be aware of what to expect and budget accordingly. For example, you will need to plan a visit to the veterinarian for vaccinations and deworming for your dog, as well as regular health check-ups. You will also need to buy food and accessories for them (bowl, cushion, etc.). Finally, budget for grooming and grooming care for your dog, if necessary.
- **Understand that adopting a dog is a long-term commitment:** It's essential to understand that adopting a dog is a long-term commitment. A Border Collie can live up to 10 to 14 years or more, and you must ensure that you are ready to take care of them throughout this period. Before adopting a Border Collie, it's important to think carefully about your decision and make sure you have everything you need to care for them properly.

By following these steps, you will be better prepared to welcome a Border Collie into your life and provide a loving home tailored to their specific needs. If you have any doubts, don't hesitate to seek advice from professionals or experienced owners of this breed.

Questions to Ask Before Adopting!

Are you ready to dedicate time and energy to physical exercise and training for your dog? Border Collies require a lot of exercise and mental stimulation to stay happy and healthy. If you are not able to play and engage in activities with your dog every day, a Border Collie might not be the right choice for you.

- **Are you willing to dedicate time and energy to physical exercise and training for your dog?** Border Collies are highly active and intelligent dogs that require regular exercise and mental stimulation to be happy.
- **Do you have experience with dogs?** Although Border Collies are intelligent, they can also be sensitive and demanding in terms of training. Previous experience with dogs can be an asset in better understanding their needs.
- **Are you willing to invest time and money in training and education for your dog?** Border Collies respond well to consistent training, but it requires time and resources. Training classes may be necessary to ensure that your dog behaves properly.
- **Are you prepared to provide constant attention to your dog?** Border Collies are very affectionate dogs and require a lot of interaction with their family. If you cannot offer this attention, this may not be the best breed for you.
- **Do you have adequate space to accommodate a dog of this size and energy?** Border Collies are medium to large-sized dogs and require enough space to move around and play. If you live in a small apartment or have limited time for walks, this may not be ideal.
- **Are you willing to accept that your dog may become noisy or destructive if their needs are not met?** Border Collies can become noisy or destructive if they get bored or don't receive enough exercise. You must be prepared to manage these behaviors.
- **Are you willing to accept the specific grooming needs of Border Collies?** The dense coat of Border Collies requires regular brushing to prevent mats and skin problems. If you're not willing to invest time in grooming, this may not be suitable.
- **Are you willing to provide quality nutrition and follow your veterinarian's recommendations for your dog's health?** Border Collies may have specific dietary needs due to their activity level. This may require an additional budget.
- **Are you willing to meet your dog's socialization needs?** Border Collies are social dogs that require interaction with other dogs and their family. If you cannot provide this, this breed may not be the best option.
- **Are you willing to monitor your dog's health and take steps to prevent potential health problems?** Border Collies can be prone to certain health conditions. This may require regular visits to the veterinarian.
- **Are you willing to dedicate time and attention to your dog despite a busy schedule?** Border Collies require constant interaction, which can be challenging if you have a very busy schedule.
- **Are you willing to adopt suitable training techniques for your Border Collie and invest in its education?** Border Collies can be sensitive and require positive and consistent training.

Answering these questions honestly will help you determine if a Border Collie is the right breed for you. Feel free to seek advice from professionals and Border Collie owners to gain a better understanding of this dog breed.

Is this the right dog breed for you?

It is crucial to ask yourself this question before adopting a purebred dog, especially a Border Collie. Border Collies are extremely intelligent and energetic dogs, originally bred for herding work. They are known for their agility, quick learning ability, and performance of complex tasks, especially in the field of livestock work. However, like all dogs, Border Collies have specific needs that must be considered before adopting one. They require plenty of exercise and mental stimulation to stay healthy and happy. Their double coat requires regular grooming to maintain its beauty and health. Border Collies are also prone to certain health conditions, and it is essential to ensure that you are willing to invest time and energy in physical exercise and maintenance for your Border Collie. You will need to invest in its health, regularly consult your veterinarian, provide quality nutrition, and offer stimulating toys and activities to prevent boredom and destructive behaviors.

If you are willing to meet these specific needs and accept the peculiarities of the Border Collie breed, then this could be an excellent choice for you. However, if you have doubts or concerns, it might be better to consider another dog breed that is better suited to your needs and lifestyle.

Here are some factors to consider before deciding if adopting a Border Collie is a good idea for you:

- **Time and Attention:** Border Collies are highly active and intelligent dogs that require a lot of time and attention for training and socialization. If you have a busy schedule, it could be challenging to manage.
- **Training and Education:** Border Collies are intelligent, but they require consistent training to be well-balanced. If you lack experience in dog training or time for training, this breed may not be the best choice for you.
- **Lifestyle:** Border Collies are highly active and require regular exercise, so a spacious yard or frequent walks are recommended. They can adapt to apartment living with sufficient exercise, but a home with outdoor space is preferable. Also, check your housing regulations regarding pets.
- **Interaction with Children:** If you have children, it's important to consider how a Border Collie will interact with them. This breed can be very affectionate toward children, but it also requires proper training and supervision.
- **Time Availability:** Border Collies require human presence and may experience separation anxiety if you are frequently absent. Are you able to spend enough time with your dog?
- **Consulting Experts:** Talk to trusted breeders, experienced Border Collie owners, dog trainers, and veterinarians for advice and information about the breed. Their knowledge can help you make an informed decision.

How to Choose a Responsible Breeder ?

Here are some tips for choosing a responsible breeder and safely acquiring a Border Collie:

- **Do Your Research:** Look for Border Collie breeders recommended by veterinarians, dog specialists, or animal welfare organizations. Check reviews and testimonials from other owners of this breed who have adopted from this breeder.
- **Demand to see the health certificates of the parents of the litter:** a responsible breeder ensures that the parents of the litter have been tested for common hereditary diseases in Border Collies. They only breed healthy dogs.
- **Visit the breeding facility:** ask to visit the place where the dogs are raised and cared for. Ensure that the Border Collies appear healthy, well-fed, and well-maintained. Check that they have enough space to move and play.
- **Ask many questions:** inquire the breeder about their breeding and training methods, how they select breeding dogs, how they handle health and behavior issues, and so on. A responsible breeder should be open, transparent, and willing to satisfactorily answer all your questions.

- **Demand an adoption contract:** a responsible breeder will provide you with an adoption contract detailing the conditions of adoption and health guarantees for your Border Collie. Make sure to carefully read this contract before signing anything.
- **Avoid breeders who hide breeding conditions or pressure you to adopt:** a responsible breeder will be happy to show you the breeding facility and answer all your questions. They should never pressure you to adopt a dog before you are ready. If a breeder refuses to show you the breeding conditions or tries to rush you, look elsewhere.
- **Beware of breeders selling puppies too young:** puppies should not be separated from their mother and litter before a minimum age of 8 weeks. A responsible breeder adheres to this rule. If a breeder tries to sell you a younger puppy, it may indicate that they are not genuinely concerned about the well-being of their dogs.
- **Avoid breeders who are not interested in your lifestyle and adoption intentions:** a responsible breeder will ensure that you are a suitable owner and that you are ready to take on all the responsibilities associated with adoption. If a breeder does not ask questions or seems disinterested in your lifestyle, it may indicate that they care more about money than finding a good home for their puppies.
- **Avoid breeders who do not offer support after adoption:** a responsible breeder should be available to answer your questions and provide support after you have adopted your dog. If a breeder does not offer this type of follow-up, it may indicate that they do not truly care about the well-being of their puppies once they are adopted.

By following these tips, you should be able to find a responsible breeder who will provide you with a healthy and well-balanced dog and will be available to support and advise you after the adoption. Keep in mind that adopting a dog is a long-term commitment, so take the time to carefully consider your decision and find the breeder that best suits your situation.

Socialization Test Before Purchase: Avoid Unpleasant Surprises.

How to choose a responsible breeder for a Border Collie? Here are some tips for selecting a trustworthy breeder and acquiring your dog safely:

- **Test Sociability Before Adoption:** Evaluate how the dog reacts in the presence of people and other dogs. Observe if it is curious and sociable or rather fearful and reserved. A curious and sociable dog will be easier to socialize and train. To perform this test, observe how the dog reacts when you approach it, talk to it, or when it is in contact with other people and other dogs. Curiosity and sociability are positive signs, while fear and reserve may require more socialization.

- **Observe External Stimulus Reactions**: Check how the dog reacts to loud noises, sudden movements, or unfamiliar objects. A calm dog that is not easily disturbed by these stimuli will be easier to train and socialize. For this test, expose the dog to various stimuli such as loud noises (e.g., clapping hands or tapping on a metallic object), sudden movements (like shaking a bottle or a paper bag), or unfamiliar objects (e.g., showing it a new toy or object). A calm reaction and ease of distraction in the presence of these stimuli are good signs, while an anxious or aggressive reaction may indicate a need for additional socialization and training.

- **Reaction to Basic Commands:** Observe how the dog responds to basic commands like "sit,"lie down," and "shake hands." A dog that quickly and easily obeys these commands will be easier to train and socialize. Test the dog using basic commands you know, and check if it executes them promptly and effortlessly. Quick obedience is a positive sign, while difficulties in obeying or understanding commands may indicate a need for additional training and socialization.

- **Obedience Test in the Presence of Distractions:** Observe how the dog responds to basic commands when distractions are present. A dog that remains focused and obeys commands even in the presence of distractions will be easier to train and socialize. For this test, introduce distractions such as loud noises, sudden movements, or unfamiliar objects while giving basic commands to the dog. The ability to stay focused and obey despite distractions is a good sign, while difficulty concentrating or obeying in the face of distractions may require additional training and socialization.

- **Assessment of Aggression:** Observe how the dog reacts to stressful or threatening situations. A calm and non-aggressive dog will be easier to train and socialize. For this test, expose the dog to stressful or threatening situations such as loud noises, sudden movements, or unfamiliar objects, and observe its reaction. A calm and non-aggressive reaction is positive, while an aggressive reaction may indicate a need for additional socialization and training to learn how to handle stress and frustration appropriately.

- **Separation Test:** Observe how the dog reacts when separated from its owners or peers. A dog that reacts calmly and without anxiety during separation will be easier to socialize and train. For this test, leave the dog alone for a limited period of time and observe its reaction. Calm and non-anxious behavior is a positive sign, while signs of anxiety or stress during separation may indicate a need for additional training and socialization to learn how to handle this situation appropriately.

These are some examples of sociability tests that you could use to assess a Border Collie before adopting it. Remember that each dog is unique, and it's important to consider all factors in your adoption decision.

The Good Dog Owner's Toolkit

There are many dog equipment options available on the market, each designed to meet specific needs or enhance your dog's life in different ways. Here are some common dog equipment items and tips to help you decide whether or not to purchase them:

1. **Leash:** a leash is essential for all dogs that are not fully trained to walk on a leash without pulling. There are several types of leashes, including regular leashes, retractable leashes, and flexible leashes. Choose a leash that suits your pet's size and strength and is comfortable for you to hold.

2. **Harness:** a harness can be a more comfortable option for your dog than walking with a leash attached to its collar. Harnesses distribute the pulling force more evenly across their body, which can be less stressful on their spine and trachea, especially if your friend is large and strong. However, it's important to choose a harness that fits well to avoid excessive or uncomfortable movement and is strong enough to withstand your dog's pulling force. It's also important not to use a harness constantly, as it can cause friction and irritation to your dog's skin.

3. **Collar and Muzzle:** a collar can be useful for attaching a leash and displaying your pet's contact information, such as their name and your phone number. It's important to choose a collar that fits your dog's size and strength and ensure that it is neither too tight nor too loose. A muzzle may be necessary, especially if your dog tends to bite or growl. It's important to choose a well-fitting muzzle to prevent it from slipping or tightening too much. However, a muzzle should not be left on your dog for extended periods of time, as it can restrict their ability to breathe and drink normally.

4. **Bed/Cushion:**

   ➢ **Basket:** more durable and easy to clean, can be used outdoors.
   ➢ **Drawback:** may be less comfortable for some dogs.
   ➢ **Cushion:** more comfortable for the dog, can be used indoors or outdoors.
   ➢ **Drawback:** may be less durable and harder to clean.

5. **Sleeping mat:** a sleeping mat can be a comfortable place for your dog to rest and relax, especially if he tends to be anxious or needs to feel secure. Make sure to choose a sleeping mat that is the right size for him and is made of comfortable and durable materials.

6. **Potty pad/litter box:**
   ➢ **Potty pad:** can be used indoors or outdoors, easy to clean.
   ➢ **Drawback:** can be costly and needs to be replaced regularly.
   ➢ **Litter box:** can be used indoors, easy to clean.
   ➢ **Drawback:** can be costly and needs to be replaced regularly.

7. **Car cushion/mat:**
   ➢ **Cushion:** more comfortable for the dog, can be used inside or outside the car.

   ➢ **Drawback:** can be less durable and harder to clean.
   ➢ **Mat:** more sturdy and easy to clean, can be cut to fit the size of your car.
   ➢ **Drawback:** can be less comfortable for the dog.

8. **Toys:** Toys can be an excellent way to mentally and physically stimulate your dog, especially if he spends a lot of time alone at home. Choose toys that are suitable for your dog's size and abilities and are made

from safe and durable materials. Avoid toys that can be easily destroyed. If your dog is of a smaller breed or has a thinner coat, it may be helpful to invest in rain or cold-weather clothing to protect him from the elements. Be sure to choose clothing that fits him well and is comfortable, allowing him to move freely.

9. **Bowls:**
   - ➤ **Stainless Steel Bowls:** Durable and easy to clean, they do not react to acidic foods or drinks.
   - ➤ **Its drawback:** can be expensive and can be noisy when the dog eats or drinks.
   - ➤ **Plastic Bowls:** lightweight and inexpensive, available in many colors and sizes.
   - ➤ **Drawback:** may be less durable and may react to acidic foods or drinks.
10. **Dog Backpack:** If you enjoy taking your dog hiking or traveling, a dog backpack can be very convenient. There are several models available, some designed to carry water and food, others designed to carry essentials like a first aid kit. Be sure to choose a backpack that is the right size for him and is comfortable for him to wear.

Border Collies tend to be more active and require more exercise, so you need to choose equipment that can withstand their energy and physical strength. Additionally, Border Collies often have hip issues, so it's important to choose a harness that supports their body without exerting excessive pressure on their hips. It's always recommended to consult with a veterinarian or a dog breeding expert for breed-specific advice before making purchases for your dog.

There are, of course, many other dog equipment options available on the market, but these are some of the most common ones. Ultimately, the decision to buy dog equipment depends on your individual needs and those of your dog. Take the time to consider what suits you best before making a purchase decision.

How to Welcome Your Dog?

The arrival of a new dog in the family is an exciting moment, but it can also be a source of stress for the animal, as it finds itself in a new environment and must adapt to new people and routines. To give your dog the best possible start in its new life with you, you need to give it your full attention and create a comfortable and secure environment. Here are some tips for structuring its welcome and education and offering it a happy and fulfilling life with you:

- ✓ **Be Patient and Calm:** when you pick up your friend from the breeder or when you welcome them into your home, they may be stressed and nervous. Give them time to adapt to their new environment and feel safe with you. Avoid overwhelming them with cuddles and affection immediately; instead, give them time to orient themselves and get used to you.
- ✓ **Create a Comfortable Space for Them:** even before bringing your Border Collie home, prepare a space for them to rest and take shelter. Provide them with a litter box, a water bowl, and a food bowl. You can also add a comfortable cushion or blanket for them to relax on.
- ✓ **Take Them Around the House and Garden:** once they are settled in their space, take them around the house and garden. Show them where the doors and windows are, the toilet area, and the other rooms in the house. This will help them better understand their surroundings and get oriented.
- ✓ **Take Time to Play and Reward Him:** playing is a very effective way to strengthen the emotional bond between you and your Border Collie. Take the time to play with them and reward them with treats when they do something good. This will help them understand what you expect from them and feel loved and appreciated.

By following these steps, you should be able to create a welcoming and comfortable environment for your new four-legged companion, allowing them to feel safe and get to know you.

How to Educate Step by Step?

Like all dogs, Border Collies can present training challenges, and it is crucial to take the time to understand their personality and needs to be able to train them effectively. Training a dog can be a challenge, but it is also a very rewarding experience for both owners and dogs. By following some simple steps and being patient and persistent, you can help your dog become well-behaved and happy. One key element of dog training is to do it positively and kindly. Dogs respond better to positive training, using words of praise and treats to reward good behavior, rather than negative or punitive methods. By being positive and encouraging with your dog, you can strengthen your relationship with them and help them become a confident and well-balanced dog.

So if you've just adopted this breed of dog and are determined to give them the best possible start by training them effectively. But you don't know how? The best methods to train them? What tips should you follow to succeed? If you're asking yourself all these questions, you're in the right place! In this part of the book, I will give you detailed advice on how to train your dog step by step, with concrete examples and tips to help you succeed. So, are you ready to become a master trainer for your new friend? Let's do it!

Here are some tips to help you get started with your dog's training:
We'll start by teaching you some rules you should follow before starting your dog's training:

⊘ Set Clear Boundaries:

You must set clear boundaries for your dog and maintain them consistently. This means you must be firm and determined when giving a command, but also fair and equitable in your treatment of your dog.

Example: set clear rules for your dog, such as "no jumping on people" or "no chewing shoes."

Here's how to do it step by step:

1. Decide on rules that will best suit your dog and your lifestyle.
2. Clearly communicate these rules to your dog using simple words and repeating commands frequently.
3. Enforce these rules consistently using a firm tone and correcting your dog when it does not follow the rules.
4. Reward your dog when you notice it follows the rules to encourage it to continue behaving desirably.

What to do if the dog refuses:

If your dog refuses to follow the rules, you can use negative correction (such as a firm "no" or leash pressure) to let them know they are behaving undesirably. Follow this correction with positive reinforcement (such as a treat or praise) when your dog behaves in a desirable manner to encourage them to continue behaving this way.

⊘ Use rewards:

Using rewards (such as treats or praise) can be an effective way to encourage your dog to learn new things and follow commands. However, it's important not to over-reward your dog as it could make them too dependent and less likely to obey without a reward.

Example: Reward your dog with a treat when they obey a command like "sit" or "lie down."

Here's how to do it step by step:

- Decide on the rewards that will work best for your dog (for example, treats or toys).
- Give your dog a clear and concise command (for example, "lie down").
- When your dog obeys the command, immediately reward them with a treat or toy.

What to do if the dog refuses:

If your dog refuses to respond to a command or perform a task, you can try to ensure they understand what you're asking, check if they are distracted or need a break, modify the reward, and gradually increase the difficulty of the task. By using these strategies, you may be able to understand why your dog is refusing to respond and find solutions to address it.

☑ Be patient:

Training a dog can take time and patience, so don't get frustrated if your dog doesn't immediately understand what you want them to do. Be patient and repeat commands consistently until your dog understands them.

Example: When teaching your dog a new command, repeat it consistently and patiently until they understand what you want them to do.

Step by step:

1. Choose a simple and easy-to-teach command (e.g., "sit").
2. Give the command clearly and concisely (e.g., "sit").
3. Wait for your dog to respond to the command. If they don't respond, repeat the command until they do.
4. When your dog responds to the command, reward them to encourage them to continue behaving this way.
5. Repeat this exercise regularly until your dog understands the command and can perform it on cue.

What to do if the dog refuses: It can be helpful to show them what you want them to do using a gesture or motion. You can also try rewarding your dog for any behavior close to what you want them to do and gradually reinforcing the requirements until they understand the full command.

☑ Be Consistent:

It's important to be consistent in how you treat your dog and give commands. If you constantly change your expectations or training methods, your dog will become confused and have difficulty learning.

Example: consistently maintain the boundaries and rules you have set for your dog, and give the same commands consistently each time you want them to do something.

Step by Step:

1. Decide on boundaries and rules that will best suit your dog and your lifestyle.
2. Clearly communicate these boundaries and rules to your dog using simple words and repeating commands frequently.
3. Enforce these boundaries and rules consistently using a firm tone and correcting your dog when they do not comply.
4. Give the same commands consistently every time you want your dog to do something. For example, always use the same word to ask them to sit (like "sit") and give the command in the same way each time.

What to do if the dog refuses: If your dog refuses to respect the boundaries or rules you have set, you can use a negative correction (like a firm "no" or leash pressure) to signal undesirable behavior. Follow this correction with positive reinforcement (like a treat or praise) when your dog behaves as desired to encourage them to continue behaving that way.

☑ Show Leadership:

It's important to show your dog that you are the leader of the pack by being firm and determined when giving commands. This means you should be in charge of food, walks, and important decisions regarding your dog's behavior.

Example: Show your dog that you are the leader of the pack by making decisions for them and being firm in your commands.

Step by Step:

- Make decisions for your dog, such as when and where they eat, sleep, and play.

- Give clear and concise commands to your dog and wait for them to perform before giving their reward.
- Be firm in your commands and use negative correction (such as a firm "no" or leash pressure) when your dog does not comply.
- Show your dog that you are the pack leader by behaving calmly and confidently and rewarding your dog when they behave in a desirable manner.

What to do if the dog refuses: If your dog refuses to follow your commands or acknowledge your leadership, it may be helpful to show them what you want them to do using a gesture or movement. You can also try progressively reinforcing the requirements until they understand the complete command.

Show Kindness:

While being firm and determined, it's important to treat your dog with kindness and show them affection. This will strengthen your relationship with them and help them feel safe and loved.

Example: Show your dog that you love and care for them by petting them, speaking to them kindly, and providing them with quality food.

Step by Step:

- Take time to pet and play with your dog every day.
- Speak to your dog in a soft and encouraging voice when you are together.
- Offer your dog high-quality food to take care of its health.
- Show your dog that you love it by giving it attention, cuddling, and hugging it.

What to do if the dog refuses: If your dog refuses to be petted or given attention, it may be helpful to respect its need for space and offer attention gradually. You can also try providing new experiences to strengthen your bond (for example, taking it for a walk in a new park or offering new toys).

Practice Positive Reinforcement:

Positive reinforcement is a training method that involves rewarding your dog when it behaves in a desirable manner. You can use treats, praise, or toys to reward your dog when it obeys a command or behaves in a desirable way.

Example: Reward your dog with a treat when it obeys a command like "sit" or "lie down."

Step by step:

- Decide on rewards that will work best for your dog (e.g., treats or toys).
- Give your dog a clear and concise command (e.g., "sit").
- When your dog obeys the command, immediately reward it with the treat or toy.
- Repeat this exercise regularly to reinforce the association between the command and the reward.

What to do if the dog refuses: if your dog refuses to respond to the command, it can be helpful to show him what you want him to do using a motion or gesture. You can also try rewarding your dog for any behavior close to what you want him to do, and then gradually reinforce the requirements until he understands the complete command.

Practice negative reinforcement exercises:

Negative reinforcement is an education method that involves using correction (such as a firm "no" or leash pressure) to signal to your dog that he is behaving undesirably. This method should be used carefully and should be followed by positive reinforcement so that your dog understands what he should do.

Example: use a firm "no" to signal to your dog that he is behaving undesirably when he jumps on people or chews on shoes.

Step by step:

- Identify your dog's undesirable behaviors (such as jumping on people or chewing on shoes).
- When your dog exhibits any of these undesirable behaviors, use a firm "no" to signal to him that he is behaving undesirably.
- Follow the negative correction with positive reinforcement (such as a treat or praise) when your dog behaves desirably to encourage him to continue behaving this way.
- Repeat this exercise regularly to reinforce the association between undesirable behavior and negative correction, and between desirable behavior and reward.

What to do if the dog refuses: If your dog continues to exhibit undesirable behavior despite negative correction, it can be helpful to show him what you want him to do using a gesture or movement. You can also try gradually reinforcing the requirements until he understands the complete command.

⊘ Do training exercises:

Training is an educational method that involves teaching your dog new skills and commands. You can use treats, praise, and toys to encourage your dog to learn new things and obey commands.

Example: Use training exercises to teach your dog new skills and to instruct them on basic commands like "sit" or "lie down."

Step by step:
- Choose a basic command to teach your dog (such as "sit" or "lie down").
- Use a movement or gesture to show your dog what you want it to do.
- Reward your dog when it performs the command correctly with a treat or praise.
- Repeat the exercise regularly until your dog understands the complete command.
- Add new basic commands over time to continue stimulating your dog's mind and strengthening its relationship with you.

What to do if the dog refuses: it can be helpful to show it what you want it to do using a movement or gesture. You can also try to gradually reinforce the requirements until it understands the complete command.

⊘ Engage in socialization exercises:

Socialization is an educational method that involves getting your dog accustomed to different people, animals, and environments. This can help your dog become less anxious and better adapt to various situations.

Example: take your dog for walks in different places and expose it to different people, animals, and environments to teach it how to behave appropriately in various situations.

Step by step:
- Take your dog for walks in different places, such as parks, shopping streets, beaches, etc.
- Gradually and in a controlled manner, expose your dog to different people, animals, and environments.
- Use rewards and praise to reinforce appropriate behavior in your dog when exposed to new situations.
- Regularly engage in socialization exercises to help your dog adapt to new situations and build confidence.

What to do if the dog refuses: If your dog displays fear or aggression when exposed to new situations, it can be helpful to remove your dog from the situation and provide a safe space for them to calm down. You can also try reducing the intensity of the situation (e.g., being farther from the source of fear) and progressively reinforcing their appropriate behavior when exposed to new situations.

⊘ Teach them to obey basic commands:

Example: teach your dog to obey basic commands like "sit,"lie down,"stay," and "come" to help them behave appropriately and obey you.

<u>**Step by step:**</u>
- ⊘ Choose a basic command to teach your dog (such as "stop" or "lie down").
- ⊘ Use a movement or gesture to show your dog what you want them to do.
- ⊘ Reward your dog when they correctly execute the command with a treat or praise.
- ⊘ Repeat the exercise regularly until your dog understands the complete command.
- ⊘ Add new basic commands over time to continue stimulating your dog's mind and strengthening your relationship with them.

<u>**What to do if the dog refuses:**</u> It may be helpful to show your dog what you want them to do using a movement or gesture. You can also try gradually reinforcing the requirements until they understand the complete command.

⊘ **Make leash walking an enjoyable moment for your dog:**

- Teach them to walk by your side without pulling on the leash. If they pull on the leash, stop and wait for them to stop pulling before resuming the walk.
- Teach them to stop when you ask using the command word "stop." If they stop when you ask, reward them with a treat and praise.

⊘ **Engage in regular physical exercise with your dog:**

<u>**Example:**</u> Walk your dog every day for at least 30 minutes to allow them to expend their energy and improve their physical fitness.

<u>**Step by Step:**</u>
1. Plan daily walks of at least 30 minutes for your dog.
2. Encourage your dog to run and play during the walk to help them expend their energy.
3. Vary the walking routes to stimulate your dog's mind.
4. If your dog has already reached its ideal physical condition, you can add additional fitness exercises such as running or jogging, canicross (running with your dog attached to you by a special leash), frisbee, fetch, and more.

<u>**What to do if the dog refuses:**</u> If your dog refuses to exercise, it can be helpful to offer rewards to motivate them to expend energy. You can also try varying the walking routes to provide new experiences and sources of stimulation.

⊘ **Be careful not to give in to your dog's whims too much:**

<u>**Example 1:**</u> If he whines for a treat, do not give him the treat until he has calmed down and obeyed a command, such as sitting or staying. If he sits and waits patiently, give him the treat and praise him for his good behavior.

<u>**Example 2:**</u> Do not give in to your dog's whims by feeding him at irregular hours or letting him sleep on your bed, as this can make him difficult to manage and lead to bad behavior.

<u>**Step by step:**</u>
- Create a regular schedule for feeding your dog and stick to it.
- Do not give your dog food or treats outside of his meal schedule.
- Do not let your dog sleep on your bed or other furniture.
- Encourage your dog to exhibit appropriate behaviors by offering rewards and praise.
- Be careful not to regularly give in to your dog's whims to help him understand who the pack leader is and to prevent him from developing bad behavior.

What to do if the dog refuses: if your dog continues to exhibit undesirable behavior despite your efforts to teach him boundaries and rules, it may be helpful to progressively reinforce the requirements until he understands what is expected of him. You can also use positive reinforcement techniques, such as rewards and praise, to encourage your dog to exhibit appropriate behavior.

⊘ Be patient and persistent in training your dog:

- Training a dog can take time and patience. Don't expect him to master all commands in a single training session.
- Be persistent and repeat the exercises every day until he masters them.
- Don't get angry if he doesn't understand immediately what you're asking for. Be patient and keep showing him how to do it. This will help strengthen your relationship with your dog and teach him appropriate behaviors.

Example 1: If he struggles to understand the "come" command, don't get angry and shout at him. Instead, use a treat to lure him to you and repeat the "come" command every time you bring him to you. Reward and praise him each time he comes to you and repeat the exercise every day until he understands the command.

Step by step:

1. Be patient when training your dog, as it can take time and effort.
2. Encourage your dog by offering rewards and praise when he successfully learns a new skill or exhibits appropriate behavior.
3. Be persistent in training your dog, even if it takes time and effort.
4. If you encounter difficulties in training your dog, don't hesitate to seek the assistance of a professional trainer.
5. Be patient and persistent in regularly training your dog to strengthen your relationship with him and teach appropriate behaviors.

What to do if the dog refuses: if your dog refuses to follow your commands or learn new skills, it can be helpful to take a break and resume training later when your dog is more relaxed and receptive. You can also try to make learning more playful and engaging for your dog by using rewards and games to motivate him.

⊘ Be consistent in training your dog.

Ensure that all family members use the same command words and reward your dog in the same way when he correctly follows a command.

Example: be consistent in training your dog by using the same command words and reinforcement techniques to teach him new skills and to help him understand boundaries and rules.

Step by Step:

1. Always use the same command words to teach him new skills.
2. Always use the same reinforcement techniques, such as rewards and praise, to encourage your dog to adopt appropriate behavior.
3. Be consistent in applying the boundaries and rules you have set for your dog.
4. Be patient and persistent in your dog's training to show him that you are his leader and you expect him to follow your commands.
5. Be consistent in your dog's training regularly to teach appropriate behaviors and strengthen your relationship with him.

What to do if the dog refuses: If your dog continues to refuse to follow your commands despite your consistency, be patient and continue to train your dog until he understands what you expect him to do. So, don't give up quickly, and remember that despite their intelligence, they are still animals that require a lot of repetition and training.

✓ Do not force your dog to do something he is not ready to do.

If he is scared or unsure of himself, give him time to get used to the situation before asking him to follow a command. **Example:** do not force your dog to do something that causes him anxiety or fear, but rather encourage him to learn at his own pace and comfort level.

Step by step:
1. Observe your dog and recognize the signs that indicate he is anxious or fearful, such as drooling, flattened ears, or avoiding eye contact.
2. Do not force your dog to do something that causes him anxiety or fear.
3. Encourage your dog to learn at his own pace and comfort level by rewarding his efforts and progress.
4. Use positive reinforcement techniques, such as rewards and praise, to encourage your dog to learn new skills.
5. Be patient and persistent in training your dog, but do not force him to do something that causes him anxiety or fear.

What to do if the dog refuses: If your dog continues to refuse to follow your commands or learn new skills, it may be helpful to take a break and resume training later when your dog is more relaxed and receptive. You can also try to make learning more fun and engaging for your dog by using rewards and games to motivate him.

Be careful not to overwork your dog.

Although they need plenty of exercise, this breed also requires time to relax and rest. Make sure to provide enough time for relaxation and rest between exercise sessions.

Example: Ensure your dog gets enough rest and relaxation time between training sessions and physical activities to avoid overworking.

Step by step:
1. Give your dog enough rest and relaxation between training sessions and physical activities.
2. Avoid overworking your dog by having it work or play for long periods of time without a break.
3. Consider your dog's age and physical condition when planning its activities and training.
4. Pay attention to signs of fatigue or overexertion in your dog, such as lethargy, loss of appetite, or difficulty concentrating.
5. If your dog shows signs of fatigue or overexertion, give them enough rest and relaxation time to recover.

What to do if the dog refuses: If your dog refuses to participate in activities or training that are usually enjoyable for them, it may be a sign that they are overworked or tired. In this case, it's important to give them enough rest and relaxation time to recover.

By following these tips, you should be able to continue your dog's education effectively and strengthen your relationship with them. Remember to always be patient and treat your dog with kindness and respect. If you have difficulty training your dog or have any questions, don't hesitate to seek the assistance of a professional trainer.

Preventive Medicine.

It is crucial to follow a preventive medicine program for your dog to protect them from diseases and parasites that can affect their health. Preventive medicine involves taking measures to prevent the occurrence of diseases in your dog. By implementing appropriate preventive medicine, you can help maintain your dog's health and well-being in the long term. Here are some tips for establishing preventive medicine for your dog:

1. **Nutrition:** providing food that is appropriate for your dog's age, weight, and needs is essential to maintain their health and prevent certain diseases.

2. **Exercise:** regular exercise is essential to maintain your dog's physical and mental fitness. Make sure to provide them with enough exercise every day through walks and playtime.
3. **Veterinary Care:** it is crucial to take your dog to the veterinarian for regular health check-ups and to get them vaccinated and dewormed according to your veterinarian's recommendations.
4. **Sterilization:** spaying or neutering your dog can help prevent certain diseases, such as breast tumors in females and prostate issues in males. Consult your veterinarian to determine if sterilization is recommended for your dog.
5. **Parasite Prevention:** internal (worms) and external (fleas, ticks) parasites can cause health problems for your dog. It is crucial to protect your dog against these parasites by providing them with deworming medication and using suitable anti-parasitic products.

By following these recommendations, you should be able to establish an effective preventive medicine routine for your pet. Feel free to seek advice from your veterinarian on how to take care of your dog's health.

Expected Veterinary Expenses!

It is necessary to understand that estimating veterinary costs for a Border Collie can vary depending on several factors. These factors include your dog's age, physical condition, overall health, required care, vaccines recommended by your veterinarian, etc. Nevertheless, here is an approximation of the annual costs you may consider for a Border Collie, taking into account the elements listed in the previous text:

- **Basic veterinary expenses (check-up consultations, vaccines, deworming, etc.):** approximately €250 to €500 per year
- **Spaying/Neutering costs:** approximately €250 to €500
- **Treatment expenses in case of illness or injury:** variable, depending on the necessary treatment
- **Cost of quality food:** approximately €100 to €200 per year
- **Grooming expenses:** approximately €50 to €100 per year
- **Transportation and travel expenses (if necessary):** variable, depending on transportation and accommodation costs

By averaging these costs, we can estimate that the veterinary expenses to anticipate for a Border Collie range from 200 to 800 euros per year. This can vary depending on your dog's health and the care it requires. Therefore, it's important to budget accordingly and consider getting health insurance for your dog if you deem it necessary. Remember that your dog's health is very important, and it's essential to provide necessary care when needed. It's also worth noting that veterinary expenses are not the only costs to consider when adopting a Border Collie. You'll also need to budget for food, accessories, and equipment (bowl, cushion, leash, collar, crate, etc.), as well as grooming and grooming care for your dog if necessary. In summary, adopting a Border Collie involves budgeting for veterinary expenses, as well as for the dog's food and maintenance. Make sure you are well aware of the needs of this dog breed and have a budget in place before deciding to adopt such a dog.

Nutrition and Feeding:

Feeding is a crucial element in maintaining your dog's health and well-being. It's essential to choose high-quality food that meets your dog's specific nutritional needs, taking into account its age, weight, activity level, and physical condition. It's also recommended to diversify meals to provide a balanced and varied diet for your dog while avoiding foods rich in fats and sugars, which can be harmful to its health.

Nutritional Needs Based on Age, Weight, and Activity Level.

Nutritional needs based on age, weight, and activity level for a Border Collie. Your Border Collie's nutritional needs vary depending on its age and activity level. Here are some factors to consider for tailored nutrition and feeding for your dog:

1. **Puppy Nutritional Needs:**

They have specific nutritional needs to support their growth and development. They require food rich in protein and calories to aid in bone and muscle development. Puppy foods should contain essential nutrients such as high-quality proteins, omega-3 and omega-6 fatty acids, vitamins, and minerals to strengthen their immune system and promote good health. They should also have an appropriate calcium/phosphorus ratio to support bone and teeth development. It is recommended to feed puppies several small meals a day rather than one or two large meals.

2. **Nutritional Needs for Adult Dogs:**

Adult dogs have different nutritional needs compared to puppies. They require a diet lower in calories and lower in poor-quality proteins to maintain optimal health and prevent obesity. However, this does not mean they don't need proteins at all, but rather they need them in lesser quantities than growing puppies. Therefore, it is crucial to choose high-quality nutrition containing good-quality proteins and other essential nutrients to support the long-term health of adult dogs.

a) **High-Quality Proteins** for dogs should provide a complete source of essential amino acids, which are the building blocks of proteins needed for growth and tissue repair. Animal-based proteins are considered a source of high-quality proteins as they contain all essential amino acids. Here are some examples of high-quality proteins for dogs: Chicken, Turkey, Beef, Lamb, Salmon, Tuna, Eggs, and Dairy Products.

b) **Poor-Quality Proteins** are typically derived from low-quality animal sources or poorly digestible plant ingredients. Here are some examples of poor-quality proteins:
   - **Animal By-Products:** these are inedible parts of animals, such as feathers, beaks, and feet, which are often used in pet foods for their protein content. However, these by-products may contain contaminants and allergens, as well as low-quality proteins.
   - **Low-Quality Meat:** some dog food brands use low-quality meat that may contain parts of sick or dead animals, hormones, and antibiotics. This meat is often hard to digest and can lead to health problems in dogs.

   - **Corn Gluten:** corn gluten is a cost-effective source of protein used in some dog foods. However, it is also poorly digestible and can cause digestive problems in some dogs.
   - **Soy:** soy is another cost-effective source of protein used in some dog foods, but it can cause allergies and digestive issues in some dogs.

It's essential to check the ingredients and protein source in dog foods to ensure they are of high quality and easily digestible for your dog. Make sure to provide superior quality food that contains essential nutrients such as proteins, fibers, healthy fats, vitamins, and minerals to support long-term health.

3. Nutritional Needs of Senior Dogs:

Senior dogs have specific nutritional needs different from puppies and adult dogs. They require an easily digestible, lower-calorie diet to maintain a healthy weight and prevent age-related health issues. Senior dog foods should contain specific nutrients such as antioxidants, omega-3 and omega-6 fatty acids, as well as fiber to support their immune system, joint health, and digestion.

4. Specific Criteria:

To determine the quantity of food and the type of diet that best suits your Border Collie, you must consider factors such as its weight, age, activity level, and individual metabolism. The calorie needs of dogs vary based on their breed, physical condition, metabolism, and other individual factors. To develop a specific diet plan for your Border Collie, always consult your veterinarian for personalized advice on feeding and nutrition.

Here is an approximate estimation of daily calorie requirements for a Border Collie based on its weight and activity level:

- **Weight: 5-10 kg;** Low activity level: 450-850 calories / Moderate activity level: 550-1000 calories / High activity level: 650-1200 calories.
- **Weight: 11-25 kg;** Low activity level: 1000-1400 calories / Moderate activity level: 1200-1800 calories / High activity level: 1500-2100 calories.
- **Weight: 26-45 kg;** Low activity level: 1700-2200 calories / Moderate activity level: 2000-2700 calories / High activity level: 2300-3200 calories.
- **Weight: 46-70 kg;** Low activity level: 2400-3000 calories / Moderate activity level: 2800-3800 calories / High activity level: 3300-4500 calories.

Note that these numbers are a general estimation, and the calorie needs of each dog may vary based on their breed, fitness level, metabolism, and other individual factors. To establish a specific dietary plan for your dog, always consult your veterinarian for tailored advice on feeding and nutrition.

Here are some tips for preparing homemade meals for your dog:

- Make sure to meet your dog's nutritional needs by providing them with an adequate source of high-quality proteins, carbohydrates, fats, vitamins, and minerals. Lean meats like chicken, turkey, and beef are good sources of proteins. Green vegetables like spinach and broccoli provide essential nutrients. Whole grains like rice and quinoa offer healthy carbohydrates. Vegetable oils such as olive oil and coconut oil provide healthy fats.
- Avoid ingredients that can be toxic to dogs, such as garlic, onions, grapes, and cherries.
- Make sure to provide an adequate amount of food to meet your dog's energy needs. An inadequate diet can lead to nutritional deficiencies and health problems.
- Consult a veterinarian or nutritionist to ensure your dog is receiving a balanced diet tailored to their specific needs. It's worth noting that preparing homemade meals for your dog can be costly and time-consuming. If you opt for commercial foods, make sure to choose a quality brand that meets the standards of the Association of American Feed Control Officials (AAFCO).

Authorized Foods

Here are some examples of homemade foods you can give to your dog:
- Lean meats such as chicken, turkey, and beef
- Green vegetables such as spinach and broccoli
- Whole grains such as rice and quinoa
- Vegetable oils such as olive oil and coconut oil
- Vegetables such as carrots, sweet potatoes, and zucchini
- Fruits such as bananas, apples, and strawberries (in small quantities)

These foods can be given to the Border Collie as a supplement to their main diet of high-quality dog kibble. It's essential to provide these fresh foods in appropriate quantities and as a complement to a balanced diet to avoid nutritional imbalances. For example, meats should be cooked and boneless, vegetables should be cooked and chopped into small pieces for easy digestion, and fruits should be given in small amounts to prevent digestive issues.

Toxic Foods.

Here is a list of foods that can be toxic or harmful to your pet:
- **Avocados:** contain a substance called persin that can be toxic to dogs, especially small dogs.
- **Onions and Garlic:** can cause hemolytic anemia in dogs, leading to fatigue, weakness, and dark-colored urine.
- **Grapes and Raisins:** can lead to kidney failure in dogs.
- **Macadamia Nuts:** can cause poisoning in dogs, resulting in muscle weakness, fever, and tremors.
- **Chocolate:** contains theobromine, which can be toxic to dogs and can cause heart problems, tremors, and diarrhea.
- **Raw Fish:** may contain parasites that can cause health problems in dogs.
- **Bones:** can splinter and shatter in your dog's stomach or intestines, leading to severe injuries or even death.
- **Tomatoes:** Tomato leaves and stems can be toxic to dogs, causing ataxia (loss of coordination) and tachycardia (rapid heart rate). Ripe tomatoes themselves are not as toxic but can cause stomach upset if consumed in large quantities.
- **Milk and Dairy Products:** Many dogs are lactose intolerant and may experience diarrhea and gas if they consume milk or dairy products.
- **Spicy Foods:** Spicy foods can cause stomach burns and diarrhea in dogs.
- **Cashews:** Cashews can cause poisoning in dogs, leading to muscle weakness, fever, and tremors.
- **Rhubarb leaves:** can be toxic to dogs, causing loss of appetite, drowsiness, and vomiting.
- **Holly leaves:** can be toxic to dogs, causing vomiting, diarrhea, tremors, and seizures.
- **Citrus fruits:** Citrus pulp and leaves can be toxic to dogs, causing vomiting, diarrhea, and liver problems.
- **Laurel leaves:** can be toxic to dogs, causing digestive disorders, drowsiness, and seizures.
- **Bell peppers:** pepper leaves can be toxic to dogs, causing vomiting and diarrhea.
- **Indoor plants:** some indoor plants, such as Spanish lily, peace lily, and lily, can be toxic to dogs and cause vomiting, diarrhea, and digestive issues.

It is prohibited to feed your dog human food that contains sugar, salt, spices, and processed ingredients as it can lead to health issues such as obesity, hypertension, and diabetes. It is also recommended to consult a veterinarian or a nutritionist before feeding homemade food to your dog to ensure you meet all of their nutritional needs.

Dry Food for Border Collie.

Dry dog food is just as important for Border Collies, but it's essential to choose high-quality kibble that perfectly meets your dog's specific nutritional needs. For your Border Collie, it is recommended to select kibble specially designed for its size and activity level. Medium to large breed dog kibble generally suits these dogs, ensuring they are rich in protein and energy. Be sure to carefully read the kibble label to ensure it contains all the essential nutrients for your dog and is suitable for its age and lifestyle.

Remember that kibble is only a part of its diet. Ensure it always has fresh, clean water available. You can also supplement its diet with fresh foods such as vegetables and meats, either as treats or as components of its main meals. Adjust portions according to its needs, maintain a nutritional balance, and remain attentive to its health and well-being.

Examples of Homemade Recipes.

Here are some examples of homemade meals you can prepare for your Border Collie:

1. Minced Meat Pâté:

Ingredients:

- 500g of minced chicken or turkey
- 1 cup of chopped vegetables (carrots, zucchini, broccoli)
- 1 egg
- 1 tablespoon of coconut oil

La préparation :

1. In a skillet, heat the coconut oil and cook the ground meat until it's well done.
2. Add the chopped vegetables and cook for another 5 minutes.
3. Add the egg and mix well.
4. Let it cool before serving.
5. Nutritional Values and Total Calories:

Tip:

You can add cooked rice or quinoa for an additional source of carbohydrates.

Nutritional Values and Total Calories:

For 100g of pâté, you will have approximately 150 calories, 18g of protein, 8g of fat, and 5g of carbohydrates.

Chicken and Rice Recipe:

Ingredients:

- 500g of chicken breasts
- 200g of brown rice
- 2 medium-sized carrots
- 2 cups of water

Preparation:

1. Cook the brown rice according to the packaging instructions.
2. Cook the chicken breasts in a pan until they are golden brown.
3. Cut the carrots into small pieces and add them to the pan with the chicken. Cook for 5 minutes.
4. Mix the chicken, carrots, and rice in a large bowl.

5. Add 2 cups of water and mix well.

You can add green vegetables such as spinach or peas for an extra dose of nutrients.

Nutritional Values and Total Calories:

Total Calories: 1080 | **Proteins:** 85 g | **Carbohydrates:** 92 g | **Fats:** 32 g

Ground Beef and Sweet Potato Recipe:

Ingredients:

- 500g of ground beef or turkey
- 200g of sweet potatoes
- 2 eggs
- 1 cup of oatmeal
- 2 tablespoons of olive oil

Preparation:

1. Preheat the oven to 180°C.
2. Peel the sweet potatoes and cut them into small pieces. Steam them until tender.
3. In a large bowl, mix the ground meat, sweet potatoes, eggs, and oatmeal.
4. Add the olive oil and mix well.
5. Shape the meatballs and place them on a baking sheet.
6. Bake in the oven for about 20 minutes or until the meatballs are golden brown.

Tip:

You can add green vegetables such as broccoli for an extra dose of nutrients.

Nutritional Values and Total Calories:

Total Calories: 1396 | Proteins: 103 g | Carbohydrates: 68 g | Fats: 78 g

Meatballs and Rice:

Ingredients:

- 500g of minced meat (beef, turkey, chicken)
- 1 cup of cooked rice
- 1 egg
- 1/2 cup of chopped vegetables (carrots, zucchini, spinach)
- 2 tablespoons of olive oil

Preparation:

1. In a large bowl, mix minced meat, cooked rice, egg, and chopped vegetables.
2. Shape the mixture into golf ball-sized meatballs.
3. In a large skillet, heat olive oil over medium heat.
4. Add the meatballs to the skillet and cook for about 10-15 minutes, turning them regularly to ensure even cooking.
5. Allow the meatballs to cool before feeding them to your dog.

Tip:

You can store the meat and rice meatballs in an airtight container in the refrigerator for about 3 days. You can also freeze them for future use.

Nutritional Values and Total Calories: This recipe contains approximately 1200 total calories, which is about 300 calories per serving (for approximately 4 servings). It is rich in protein, fiber, and vitamins due to the added vegetables. Remember to consider this recipe in your dog's daily ration.

Chicken and Vegetable Muffins

Ingredients:

- 2 cups whole wheat flour
- 2 teaspoons baking powder
- 1 cup cooked and chopped chicken
- 1 cup chopped vegetables (carrots, zucchini, spinach)
- 1 egg
- 1/4 cup olive oil
- 1 cup water

Preparation:

1. Preheat your oven to 180°C and grease a muffin tin.
2. In a large bowl, mix whole wheat flour and baking powder.
3. Add chopped chicken, chopped vegetables, egg, olive oil, and water to the bowl and mix well.
4. Pour the mixture into the muffin tin, filling each muffin cup two-thirds full.
5. Bake the muffins for about 20-25 minutes, or until they are golden and a toothpick comes out clean.
6. Allow the muffins to cool before giving them to your dog.

Tip: You can store the chicken and vegetable muffins in an airtight container in the refrigerator for about 5 days. You can also freeze them for future use.

Nutritional Values and Total Calories: This recipe contains approximately 1600 calories in total, which is about 200 calories per muffin (for about 8 muffins). It is rich in proteins, fibers, and vitamins thanks to the added vegetables. Don't forget to consider this recipe in your dog's daily ration.

Beef and Brown Rice Meatballs

Ingredients:

- 500g of lean ground beef
- 1 cup of cooked brown rice
- 1 egg
- 1 cup of chopped vegetables (carrots, spinach, zucchini)
- 1/4 cup of fresh chopped parsley
- 1 tablespoon of olive oil

Preparation:

1. Preheat your oven to 180°C.
2. In a large bowl, mix the ground beef, cooked brown rice, egg, chopped vegetables, and fresh chopped parsley.
3. Shape the mixture into golf ball-sized meatballs and place them on a baking sheet lined with parchment paper.
4. Brush the meatballs with olive oil.
5. Bake the beef and brown rice meatballs in the oven for about 25-30 minutes, or until they are golden brown and cooked through.

6. Allow the meatballs to cool before giving them to your dog.

Tip: You can store the beef and brown rice meatballs in an airtight container in the refrigerator for about 5 days. You can also freeze them for future use.

Nutritional Values and Total Calories: This recipe contains approximately 1300 calories in total, or about 100 calories per meatball (for approximately 13 meatballs). It is rich in protein due to the beef and in fiber and vitamins due to the added vegetables. Don't forget to consider this recipe in your dog's daily allowance.

Chicken and Rice Broth

Ingredients:

- 2 chicken thighs
- 1 cup of uncooked white rice
- 4 cups of water
- 2 carrots, cut into small pieces
- 2 celery stalks, cut into small pieces
- 1 tablespoon of olive oil

Preparation:

1. In a large pot, heat the olive oil over medium heat.
2. Add the chicken thighs and brown on all sides.
3. Add the carrots and celery, then pour the water into the pan.
4. Bring everything to a boil, then reduce the heat and simmer for about 30 minutes, or until the chicken is cooked through and tender.
5. Remove the chicken thighs from the pot and allow to cool before removing the meat from the bones and cutting into small pieces.
6. Add the uncooked white rice to the pot, then return the chicken meat to the pot.
7. Simmer for about 20 minutes, or until the rice is cooked.
8. Let the broth cool before serving it to your dog.

Tip: You can store the chicken and rice broth in an airtight container in the refrigerator for about 5 days. You can also freeze the broth for future use.

Nutritional Values and Total Calories: This recipe contains approximately 1500 calories in total, which is about 250 calories per serving (for about 6 servings). It is rich in protein thanks to the chicken and carbohydrates from the rice. It also contains vitamins and minerals from the added vegetables. Don't forget to consider this recipe in your dog's daily diet.

Meatballs and Vegetables

Ingredients:

- 500g minced meat (chicken, turkey, or beef)
- 2 grated carrots
- 1 grated zucchini
- 1 cup of oatmeal
- 1 egg
- 1 tablespoon olive oil

La preparación:

1. In a large bowl, combine ground beef, grated carrots, grated zucchini, oatmeal and egg.

2. Mix well until all ingredients are well incorporated.
3. Form meatballs the size of a golf ball with the meat and vegetable mixture.
4. In a large skillet, heat olive oil over medium heat.
5. Add the meatballs and vegetables to the skillet and cook for approximately 10 to 15 minutes, or until cooked through.
6. Allow the meatballs and vegetables to cool before serving to your dog.

Tip: You can store the meat and vegetable meatballs in an airtight container in the refrigerator for about 5 days. You can also freeze the meatballs for future use.

Nutritional Values and Total Calories: This recipe contains approximately 1200 calories in total, which is about 200 calories per serving (for about 6 servings). It is rich in protein due to minced meat and fiber due to vegetables and oats. It also contains vitamins and minerals due to the added vegetables. Don't forget to consider this recipe in your dog's daily ration.

Sweet Potato and Oat Biscuits

Ingredients:

- 1 medium-sized sweet potato, peeled and cut into small cubes
- 1 cup of oats
- 1/4 cup of whole wheat flour
- 1/4 cup of natural peanut butter (no added sugar)
- 1 egg

Preparation:

1. Preheat the oven to 180°C (356°F).
2. In a saucepan, bring water to a boil and add the sweet potato cubes. Cook until they are tender, about 10 to 15 minutes.
3. In a large bowl, mix the oats, whole wheat flour, peanut butter, and egg until all the ingredients are well incorporated.
4. Add the cooked sweet potato cubes to the bowl and mix well until they are fully incorporated into the dough.
5. Shape biscuits using your hands or a cookie cutter. Place them on a baking sheet lined with parchment paper.
6. Bake the biscuits for approximately 25 minutes, or until they are golden and firm.
7. Allow the biscuits to cool completely before giving them to your dog.

Tip: You can store the sweet potato and oat biscuits in an airtight container in the refrigerator for about a week. You can also freeze them for future use.

Nutritional Values and Total Calories: This recipe contains approximately 800 calories in total, which is about 100 calories per biscuit (for about 8 biscuits). It is rich in fiber thanks to the sweet potato and oatmeal, and in protein thanks to peanut butter and egg. It also contains vitamins and minerals thanks to the sweet potato. Don't forget to consider this recipe in your dog's daily allowance.

Chicken and Sweet Potato Meatballs

Ingredients (for about 20 meatballs):

- 500g of ground chicken
- 200g of grated sweet potato
- 2 beaten eggs
- 50g of oatmeal

- 1 tablespoon of coconut oil

Preparation:

1. Preheat the oven to 180°C.
2. In a large bowl, mix the ground chicken, grated sweet potato, beaten eggs, and oatmeal.
3. Shape the mixture into ping pong-sized balls.
4. In a medium skillet, heat the coconut oil over medium heat.
5. Add the chicken balls and brown them on all sides.
6. Place the balls on a baking sheet and bake them in the oven for about 20 minutes.

Tip: You can add additional vegetables, such as grated carrots or zucchini, to increase the nutrient content of the recipe.

Nutritional Values and Total Calories:

- Calories: 60 calories per ball | Protein: 6 g | Carbohydrates: 2 g | Fat: 3.5 g

Important: It should be noted that these examples of homemade meals are for reference purposes and may not cover all of your dog's nutritional needs. It is recommended to consult with a veterinarian or nutritionist before feeding homemade food to ensure that you meet all of their nutritional requirements.

Your Dog's Health:

Border Collies are energetic and resilient dogs that require care and attention to stay healthy at every stage of their life. Understanding their health and care needs is essential to keep them in good shape and happy throughout their existence. In this section, we will explore in detail the health and care needs at each stage of their life, from puppy to adult, and to the senior dog.

Common Diseases and Their Prevention

Like all dogs, Border Collies can be prone to certain diseases. Here is a non-exhaustive list of conditions that can affect Border Collies:

1. Hip Dysplasia:

Hip dysplasia is an inherited condition characterized by abnormal hip development, which can lead to pain and mobility issues. To prevent hip dysplasia, it's crucial to choose dog parents that have been tested for this condition and maintain an optimal weight for your dog. Border Collies are particularly predisposed to this disease, so it's essential to monitor their weight and provide them with a high-quality diet to preserve joint health.

2. Skin Problems:

Border Collies can be prone to various skin issues, such as allergies, fungal infections, and parasites. To prevent these problems, it is recommended to maintain good hygiene by regularly brushing your dog's coat and bathing them with a shampoo suitable for their skin. Also, regularly check your dog's skin for any potential issues.

3. Thyroid Disorders:

The thyroid plays a crucial role in your dog's metabolism and overall body function. Thyroid problems can be caused by an insufficient or excessive production of thyroid hormones, leading to issues with weight, skin, and coat. To prevent these problems, have your dog's thyroid regularly tested by your veterinarian and follow recommendations to maintain their thyroid health.

4. Heart Diseases:

Border Collies can be predisposed to certain heart diseases, such as dilated cardiomyopathy. To prevent these problems, ensure that your dog's heart health is regularly monitored by your veterinarian, and follow their recommendations to maintain their heart health. Vaccinate your dog against heart diseases and monitor their weight by providing appropriate nutrition and enough exercise. Avoid foods harmful to their heart, such as chocolate.

5. Ear Infections:

Border Collies have upright ears that are less prone to infections than floppy ears. However, it's essential to regularly clean your dog's ears to prevent infections and monitor any potential irritation or infection. Use an ear cleaner suitable for their breed and consult your veterinarian if you observe signs of ear infection or irritation in your dog.

6. Eye Diseases:

Border Collies can be prone to various eye conditions, such as cataracts and glaucoma. To prevent these issues, regularly monitor your Border Collie's eye health, and if you notice any abnormalities, consult your veterinarian for proper diagnosis and treatment.

Border Collies are energetic and intelligent dogs that require attentive care to stay healthy at every stage of their life. Understanding their health and care needs is crucial to keep them fit and happy throughout their existence. In this section, we will explore in detail the specific health requirements at each stage of your Border Collie's life, from puppyhood to adulthood and beyond.

7. Brain Diseases:

Border Collies can be susceptible to certain brain diseases, such as epilepsy. To prevent these issues, regularly monitor your dog's health, and make sure to have them vaccinated against recommended brain diseases. Also, avoid leaving your dog unattended in places where they might bump their head, such as near pools or open windows at head height.

8. Bladder Diseases:

Border Collies can be prone to bladder infections and urinary stones. To prevent these problems, maintain good urinary hygiene for your dog and provide them with a diet suitable for their breed. Encourage your dog to drink enough water and urinate regularly. Offer them a balanced diet with an appropriate amount of protein, and avoid foods that can cause urinary issues, such as bones and fatty foods.

9. Liver Diseases:

Border Collies can be prone to liver diseases, such as hepatitis and hepatic steatosis. To prevent these issues, regularly monitor your dog's liver health and provide them with a diet suitable for their breed. Avoid giving your dog fatty or calorie-rich foods.

10. Cancer:

Border Collies, like all dogs, can be prone to cancer. To prevent cancer, regularly monitor your dog's health and have them vaccinated against diseases that can increase their risk of developing cancer, such as hepatitis and feline leukemia viruses.

11. Hypoglycemia:

Hypoglycemia can also be a concern for Border Collies, especially puppies and elderly dogs. Like all dogs, this condition is characterized by low blood sugar levels, which can lead to weakness, drowsiness, and even seizures. To prevent hypoglycemia, it's important to feed your dog regularly with a diet suitable for their breed and monitor for any signs of weakness or lethargy. Consult your veterinarian for specific dietary and care recommendations to prevent hypoglycemia in your Border Collie.

Explanation:

Just like in humans, your dog's blood sugar level is regulated by insulin, a hormone produced by the pancreas. When they eat, the sugar in their food is absorbed by the digestive tract and enters the bloodstream. Insulin then regulates the sugar level by facilitating its entry into cells, where it's used as a source of energy. If the blood sugar level is too high, the pancreas produces insulin to lower it. If the blood sugar level is too low, the pancreas produces glucagon, another hormone that releases stored sugar from the liver and muscles.

Foods that can disrupt blood sugar levels, such as those high in sugars or fats, or containing low-quality ingredients, can disturb your dog's metabolism and impair its ability to regulate its sugar levels. If your dog regularly consumes such foods, its blood sugar levels can become unstable, increasing the risk of hypoglycemia. This can lead to severe symptoms such as weakness, drowsiness, tremors, seizures, or coma, and must be promptly treated by a veterinarian.

Prevention:

Here are some ways to prevent hypoglycemia in your dog:

- **Feed your dog regular meals:** ensure that you provide your dog with a regular and balanced diet, following the quantities recommended by your veterinarian or a nutritionist.
- **Avoid foods that can disrupt blood sugar levels:** avoid giving your dog foods that can disrupt its blood sugar levels, such as foods high in sugars or fats, or foods containing low-quality ingredients.
- **Monitor your dog's exercise:** ensure that your dog does not overexert itself during exercise, providing it with moderate physical activity tailored to its level of fitness.
- **Be alert to signs of hypoglycemia:** monitor your dog and pay attention to signs of hypoglycemia, such as weakness, drowsiness, trembling, seizures, or coma. If you notice these signs, seek advice from your veterinarian.

How to Prevent Obesity?

It is difficult to give a general answer to this question because the ideal weight of a dog depends on several factors such as its breed, size, age, and activity level. However, there is a simple way to determine if your dog is overweight or obese: you can feel it.

To do this, place your hand on your dog's back with your thumb on one of its ribs and your fingers on the other. You should be able to feel your dog's ribs under a thin layer of fat, but they should not be visible or easily palpable. If you cannot feel your dog's ribs, it likely means that it is overweight or obese.

Obesity is a health problem that can affect dogs of all breeds, including Border Collies. Although this breed is generally active and athletic, obesity can still occur if it receives inadequate nutrition or lacks exercise and mental stimulation. Obesity can lead to serious health issues such as joint problems, heart disorders, and a reduced lifespan. To prevent obesity in your dog.

Here are some tips to prevent obesity in your dog:

- **Choose high-quality and nutritionally appropriate food for your dog:** select food that contains high-quality ingredients and meets your dog's nutritional needs. Avoid fatty and sugary foods that can contribute to obesity.
- **Follow the recommended portions:** provide your dog with portions suitable for its needs to avoid overfeeding. Consult your veterinarian or the packaging of the food for recommended portions.
- **Avoid giving too many treats and "snacks" to your dog:** while it may be tempting to reward your dog with food, excessive "treats" can contribute to obesity if given in large quantities.

- **Provide regular exercise for your dog:** offer your pet daily walks and playtime to help them expend energy and maintain their physical fitness.
- **Monitor your dog's weight:** regularly weigh your dog to ensure they are not gaining excessive weight. If you notice weight gain, you can adjust their food intake or increase their exercise level.

By following these tips, you should be able to prevent obesity in your dog. Feel free to seek advice from your veterinarian or an animal nutritionist if you have any doubts about your dog's diet or exercise. By maintaining a healthy weight for your dog, you are contributing to their long-term health and well-being.

How to Prevent Diabetes?

It's possible for your dog to suffer from diabetes, just like any other dog breed. Diabetes is a metabolic disease characterized by insufficient production of insulin by the pancreas or poor utilization of insulin by the body. This deficiency can lead to high levels of sugar in the blood (hyperglycemia) and serious health complications if not adequately treated.

Clinical signs of diabetes in dogs may include:
- Excessive thirst and frequent urination
- Weight loss despite a normal or increased appetite
- Weakness and fatigue
- Blurred vision or loss of vision
- Irritability or behavior changes

The exact causes of diabetes in dogs:
The exact causes of diabetes in dogs are not fully understood. However, certain factors have been shown to increase the risk of developing this disease:
- **Being overweight or obese:** Overweight or obesity can disrupt carbohydrate metabolism and increase the risk of diabetes.
- **Leading a sedentary lifestyle:** Dogs that lack exercise are more prone to developing diabetes than active ones.
- **Having an inadequate diet:** A diet rich in carbohydrates and calories can increase the risk of diabetes in dogs.
- **Having a family history of diabetes:** Some dogs may have a genetic predisposition to diabetes.
- **Some medications:** Some medications can interfere with insulin metabolism and increase the risk of diabetes.

Prevention: You must monitor your dog for any signs of diabetes and consult your veterinarian if you have concerns. Diabetes is a serious disease that requires lifelong treatment, but it can be effectively managed with proper nutrition, exercise, and medications prescribed by your veterinarian.

Recommendations:

- **Choose appropriate nutrition:** Feeding your dog appropriate to their needs can help prevent diabetes. Consult your veterinarian or an animal nutritionist to choose the right diet for your dog. For example, if they have a high risk of developing diabetes, you can opt for a low-carbohydrate and moderate-protein diet.

- **Follow recommended portions:** Make sure to provide your dog with portions that match their calorie needs. You can refer to the packaging information or consult your veterinarian for the recommended portions for your dog. For example, if your dog needs 500 calories a day, you can give them a cup of food containing 250 calories in the morning and another cup containing 250 calories in the evening. (Don't forget to refer to the "Nutrition and Feeding" chapter to know the portions to give your dog).

Hypertension, also known as high blood pressure, is a medical condition in which blood pressure (the force exerted by blood on the walls of blood vessels) is elevated. Hypertension can be dangerous for dogs as it can lead to damage to blood vessels and organs, as well as heart, kidney, and eye problems. It is possible that your dog may suffer from hypertension, although this condition is generally more common in older dogs or those with certain diseases (such as diabetes).

Clinical signs of hypertension may include:
1. Dilated pupils
2. Weight loss
3. Weakness or fatigue
4. Vomiting
5. Edema (swelling of limbs)

Les causes exactes de l'hypertension :
The exact causes of hypertension in dogs are not fully understood. However, it has been shown that certain medical conditions and risk factors can increase the risk of developing this condition:
1. **Being older:** Hypertension is more common in older dogs.
2. **Having certain diseases:** Some diseases, such as diabetes, kidney disease, and heart disease, can increase the risk of hypertension.
3. **Being overweight or obese:** Overweight or obesity can increase blood pressure.
4. **Having a sedentary lifestyle:** Dogs who lack exercise are more prone to developing hypertension than those who are active.
5. **Taking certain medications:** Some medications, such as corticosteroids and angiotensin-converting enzyme (ACE) inhibitors, can increase blood pressure.

Here are some tips to prevent hypertension in your dog:
- **Monitor your dog's blood pressure:** Your veterinarian can measure your dog's blood pressure during health check-ups. If your dog has high blood pressure, your veterinarian may recommend treatments to lower it.
- **Follow your veterinarian's treatment recommendations:** If medications have been prescribed to lower your dog's blood pressure, make sure to give them as directed by your veterinarian. For example, if your veterinarian has recommended giving your dog a lisinopril tablet every morning, be sure to follow that prescription.
- **Provide your dog with regular physical activity:** Regular exercise can help lower your dog's blood pressure. Offer daily walks and playtime so that your dog can expend energy. For example, you can take him for long walks, play frisbee with him, or provide interactive toys that require physical effort.
- **Promote a healthy diet:** A healthy diet that includes quality ingredients and is rich in fruits and vegetables can help lower your dog's blood pressure. Avoid fatty and salty foods that can contribute to hypertension. For example, you can include vegetables like carrots, spinach, and peas in his diet.

By following these tips, you should be able to prevent hypertension in your pet. Don't hesitate to seek advice from your veterinarian or an animal nutritionist for more personalized recommendations.

How to Measure Your Dog's Blood Pressure at Home:
I can provide you with criteria to consider when choosing a blood pressure measurement device for your dog:

- **Size of the Device:** choose a device that is suitable for your dog's size. Blood pressure measurement devices for dogs are available in different sizes to accommodate different dog breeds.
- **Ease of Use:** opt for a device that is easy to use and understand to avoid errors in measuring your dog's blood pressure.
- **Accuracy:** choose a device that is accurate and reliable. You can check online user reviews to get an idea of the device's accuracy.
- **Compatibility:** check that the device is compatible with your computer or phone for easy tracking of your dog's blood pressure measurement results.
- **Brand:** choose a device made by a well-known brand known for its quality and reliability.

Here are the steps to follow to measure your dog's blood pressure at home:

1. First, make sure your dog is calm and relaxed. You can pet him or speak to him softly to help him relax.
2. Choose a quiet and comfortable place to take the measurement, for example, in a calm room.
3. Place the cuff around your dog's front leg, just above his elbow. Ensure that the cuff is snug but not too tight to avoid affecting blood circulation.
4. Turn on the measuring device and follow the manufacturer's instructions to measure blood pressure.
5. Read the results and record them in a notebook or a health tracking app for your dog.

It's important to note that measuring blood pressure in dogs can be challenging to do correctly without prior training or experience. Therefore, it is recommended to seek advice from your veterinarian before attempting to measure your dog's blood pressure at home.

Signs of Good Health.

Here are some concrete examples of signs that may indicate your dog is in good health:

1. **Normal Appetite:** A healthy dog typically has a normal appetite and eats regularly. If your dog has lost appetite or is eating more or less than usual, it can be a sign of health issues.
2. **Robustness:** A healthy dog has well-maintained skin and fur, without open wounds or visible parasites.
3. **Good Digestion:** A healthy dog has normal bowel movements and is not constipated or experiencing diarrhea.
4. **Proper Hydration:** A healthy dog drinks an adequate amount of water and does not have a dry tongue or sunken eyes.
5. **Normal Energy:** A healthy dog has a normal energy level for its breed and age. If your dog is slower or less active than usual, it can be a sign of health problems.
6. **Normal Behavior:** A healthy dog exhibits normal behavior for its breed and age. If your dog is irritable or has unusual changes in behavior, it can be a sign of health problems.
7. **Fresh Breath:** A healthy dog has normal breath and does not have bad breath or unusual mouth odor.
8. **Good Vision and Hearing:** A healthy dog has good vision and hearing, without signs of vision loss or deafness.
9. **Good Mobility:** A healthy dog has good mobility and does not show signs of pain or difficulty in moving.

10. **Normal Body Temperature:** A healthy dog has a normal body temperature, typically ranging between 38 and 39 degrees Celsius.

You should monitor your dog for any signs of health problems and consult your veterinarian if you have any concerns. Regularly monitoring your dog's health can help detect health issues early and treat them effectively. This may include follow-up visits to the veterinarian, blood tests, and X-rays, as well as keeping an eye on your dog for any signs of health problems. By taking proactive care of your dog and following your veterinarian's recommendations, you can help maintain their good health and provide them with an optimal quality of life.

Signs That Should Alert You

There are several signs that can alert you that your dog is not in good health and should prompt you to consult a veterinarian. Here are some examples:

1. **Loss of Appetite:** If your dog loses its appetite or eats less than usual, it can be a sign of health problems. For example, an infection, inflammation, or pain can all cause a loss of appetite in a dog.
2. **Changes in Stool or Urine:** Soft, diarrheal, or constipated stools, or an increase or decrease in urination frequency, can be signs of health problems. For example, an infection, inflammation, or kidney disease can all cause changes in stool or urine.

Changes in a dog's stool or urine can indicate an abnormality, infection, or illness. Here are some signs to watch for:

Changes in Stool:
- **Diarrhea:** frequent and liquid stools
- **Constipation:** hard and difficult-to-pass stools
- **Presence of Blood in Stools:** may indicate an infection or inflammation in the intestines
- **Black and Tarry Stools:** may indicate bleeding in the stomach or intestines
- **Pale Stools:** may indicate a liver or gallbladder problem

Urine Changes:
- **Dark Urine:** may indicate dehydration or a kidney problem
- **Clear Urine:** may indicate excessive urination or excessive water consumption
- **Presence of Blood in Urine:** may indicate a urinary tract infection or inflammation
- **Urinary Incontinence:** involuntary loss of urine, may indicate a bladder or sphincter control problem
- **Increased Urination Frequency:** may indicate a urinary tract infection or kidney disease

You should monitor your dog's stools and urine and consult a veterinarian if you notice changes in their appearance, frequency, or odor.

3. **Weight Loss:** Sudden or significant weight loss can be a sign of health problems. For example, illness, infection, or organ failure can all cause weight loss.
4. **Behavior Changes:** Unusual behavior changes, such as irritability, agitation, or lethargy, can be signs of health problems. For example, pain, infection, or mental illness can all cause behavior changes.

Here are some examples of behavior changes that can be signs of health problems in a dog:

- **Irritability or Aggression:** If your dog suddenly becomes more irritable or aggressive, it may be a sign of physical or mental discomfort or pain. It is important to consult a veterinarian to rule out any underlying medical causes.
- **Lethargy:** If your dog is unusually calm and lethargic, it may be a sign of an underlying illness or health problem. You should carefully monitor your dog's other signs and symptoms of illness.
- **Changes in Appetite:** If your dog suddenly loses appetite or eats more than usual, it may be a sign of an underlying illness or health problem.
- **Changes in Urination or Bowel Habits:** If your dog starts urinating or defecating in unusual places or shows signs of pain or discomfort during these activities, it may indicate a health problem.
- **Changes in Sleep Patterns:** If your dog has trouble sleeping, wakes up frequently, or seems to have restless sleep, it may be a sign of an underlying health problem.
- **Changes in Activity Levels:** If your dog suddenly becomes less active or less interested in activities it used to enjoy, it may be a sign of an underlying illness or health problem.

5. **Injuries or lesions:** Injuries or lesions that do not heal or worsen can be a sign of health problems. For example, an infection, a skin condition, or a tumor can all cause injuries or lesions that do not heal.
6. **Bad breath or unusual mouth odor:** Bad breath or unusual mouth odor can be signs of health problems, such as infections or dental issues.
7. **Changes in coat or skin:** Changes in coat or skin, such as dull coat, shedding, or dry and irritated skin, can be signs of health problems, such as allergies, parasites, or thyroid issues.
8. **Coughing, sneezing, or other respiratory problems:** Coughing, sneezing, or other respiratory problems can be signs of health problems, such as infections, allergies, or heart diseases.
9. **Pain or discomfort:** Pain or discomfort, such as whining, crying, or difficulty moving, can be signs of health problems, such as painful joints, infections, or back issues.

You should monitor your dog for any signs of health problems and consult your veterinarian if you have concerns. Early treatment can help effectively manage many health issues and maintain overall good health.

What temperature can a Border Collie tolerate?

The Border Collie is a dog breed originating from Scotland, originally bred for herding work in often harsh conditions. As a result, this breed is well suited to relatively cold temperatures. However, each dog is unique, and their ability to tolerate specific temperatures depends on several factors, including their coat, activity level, age, overall health, and adaptation to the environment.

In general, a healthy adult Border Collie can typically tolerate temperatures ranging from 0 to 30 degrees Celsius, provided that appropriate precautions are taken to protect them from extreme heat or cold. Here are some tips to help your Border Collie cope with different weather conditions:

1. **In cold weather:**
   - Ensure your Border Collie has a warm and dry shelter with comfortable bedding, especially at night.
   - When temperatures are very cold, consider having your dog wear a coat or jacket to protect them from the cold.
   - Avoid prolonged periods of exposure to the cold, especially if your dog is wet.
2. **In hot weather:**
   - Ensure your Border Collie has access to fresh and clean water at all times.

- Avoid exercising during the hottest hours of the day; opt for early morning or late evening walks instead.
- Never leave your dog in a hot car, even if the windows are partially open.

Remember that your dog's adaptation to temperatures can vary, and you should closely observe your Border Collie for any signs of overheating or discomfort in hot weather, or shivering in cold weather. Consult your veterinarian if you have concerns about your dog's ability to handle temperatures in your area.

Basic Care

Border Collies are intelligent and energetic dogs that require care and attention to stay healthy at every stage of their lives. Here are the health and care needs to consider for each stage of your Border Collie's life:

When They're a Puppy:

- ✔ **Vaccinations:** Puppies require several vaccinations to protect them from common diseases and infections. Your veterinarian will recommend a vaccination schedule tailored to your puppy's age and needs.
- ✔ **Deworming:** Puppies need deworming to eliminate internal parasites such as intestinal worms. Your veterinarian will recommend a deworming schedule tailored to your puppy's age and needs.
- ✔ **Spaying or Neutering:** If you do not plan to breed your dog, consider spaying or neutering. This can help prevent certain diseases and undesirable behaviors.
- ✔ **Training and Socialization:** Puppies require proper training and socialization to become well-balanced dogs. Enroll your puppy in training classes and arrange social meetings with other dogs and people.
- ✔ **Nutrition:** Large breed puppies like Border Collies have specific nutritional needs. Provide appropriate nutrition to avoid growth problems.

When They Are Adults:

For an adult dog, the same health and care needs apply. Here are some details to consider for each stage of your dog's life:
- ✔ **Diet:** Ensure you provide a balanced diet based on their size, weight, and activity level.
- ✔ **Vaccinations:** Keep their vaccinations up to date to protect them from common illnesses. Your veterinarian will advise you on the appropriate vaccination schedule.
- ✔ **Deworming:** Perform regular deworming treatments to eliminate internal parasites.
- ✔ **Dental Care:** Ensure regular dental care to prevent dental problems. This may include tooth brushing and professional cleanings.
- ✔ **Exercise and Physical Activity:** Ensure that they get enough exercise to maintain their physical and mental health. Daily walks and stimulating activities are essential.
- ✔ **Health:** Specifically monitor their joint health, as Border Collies can be prone to certain conditions..

When it's Elderly:

When it's elderly, this breed also requires additional care to maintain its health and well-being. Here are some of the health and care needs to consider for each stage of your dog's life:

- ✔ **Veterinary Visits:** Senior dogs require more frequent vet visits to monitor their health and detect any issues early on.

- ✔ **Dental Care:** Dental issues can be more common in elderly dogs, so ensure regular dental care.
- ✔ **Appropriate Diet:** Choose a diet that suits the needs of your senior dog by consulting your veterinarian.
- ✔ **Moderate Exercise:** Provide moderate walks and activities suitable for their energy level and mobility.
- ✔ **Health:** Prevent mobility and arthritis issues by providing exercise suitable for their health condition.

A care program tailored to each stage of your Border Collie's life is essential to ensure their long-term well-being. Discuss any questions or concerns about your dog's care and health with your veterinarian. With the right care, you can help your furry friend lead a happy and healthy life.

Grooming and Complete Care.

Grooming and complete care for a Border Collie include several important elements to maintain your dog's health and appearance. These care routines involve grooming the coat, teeth, claws, ears, and face. It is recommended to have your Border Collie groomed by a trusted professional to ensure that the care is done properly and safely, or you can learn to do them yourself by following the detailed steps in this book. These care routines can be costly, but they are essential to maintain your dog's health and appearance.

What Do I Need?

Here is the list of tools you should have to take care of your Border Collie:
- ✔ **Gentle Brush:** to brush your dog's fur and remove dead hair. Choose the brush that suits your Border Collie's coat. They have a double coat, with a dense undercoat and longer guard hairs. A pin brush or a Furminator brush can be used to remove dead hair and tangles more easily.
- ✔ **Dog Shampoo:** to give your dog a bath and keep its skin and coat healthy. How to choose a good shampoo for a Border Collie? The main qualities recommended for a good dog shampoo are as follows:
  - Cleansing and lightweight (non-irritating);
  - pH in the range of 5.5 to 7.2, which will be close to that of the Border Collie's skin;
  - Regulator of sebum and skin grease production (when necessary);
  - Anti-bacterial, anti-fungal, antiparasitic; and moisturizing is mandatory.
- ✔ **Dog Toothbrush:** to clean your dog's teeth and prevent dental problems.
- ✔ **Dog Toothpaste:** to help clean your dog's teeth and prevent dental problems.

> **Good to know:** if using a human toothbrush is tolerated, never use your toothpaste for a dog. Human toothpaste is very unpleasant for the dog and is not designed to be ingested at all. As a result, your dog may suffer from significant digestive problems.

- • **Nail Clippers:** to safely trim your dog's nails. Border Collie's nails are thicker and harder than those of other dogs, so it's important to use nail clippers suitable for their size and thickness.

Grooming the Coat:

The Border Collie has a double thick and straight coat that requires regular maintenance to prevent knots and tangles. Grooming the coat may also include trimming the hair around the paws, tail, and ears.

What brush should I choose?

The Border Collie has a medium-length and dense coat that requires an appropriate brush to maintain its health and appearance. The recommended brush is a firm bristle brush or an undercoat brush. The firm bristle brush helps remove dead hair and untangle knots, while the undercoat brush helps remove dead hair and reduce the amount of shedding. It is also recommended to use a detangling brush to remove knots and tangles without harming your dog's skin. Regularly brushing your Border Collie is necessary to keep its coat healthy and prevent issues like knots and matted fur.

There are several types of brushes for long-haired dogs like the Border Collie. Here are the most common ones:
- ✔ **The Slicker Brush:** It helps remove dead hair and smooth the coat.
- ✔ **The Furminator Brush:** It helps remove dead hair deeply and prevents the formation of knots.
- ✔ **The Rubber Brush:** It is ideal for massaging your dog's skin and removing dead hair.

Brush your dog regularly:
- ✔ Brush your Border collie at least once a week to remove dead hair and maintain its fur's health.
- ✔ Use an appropriate brush to avoid injuring its skin.

✔ During brushing, also check your dog's ears, eyes, and paws to ensure there are no health issues or parasites.

Here's how to perform this care in detail:
1. Before you start grooming your dog, begin by brushing it to remove dead hair and knots.
2. Start with the head and work your way down your dog's body, going through the chest, belly, and legs.
3. Brush your dog's ears by gently lifting them and softly brushing the hair inside.
4. Brush your dog's paws by lifting them and gently brushing the hair between the toes.

Brushing Short and Medium-Haired Dogs:
✔ To brush a short or medium-haired dog, it is recommended to start by using a fine-tooth comb to check for any knots. This helps locate the areas where the hair is most tangled and address them first.
✔ Next, it is advisable to use a moisturizing product such as coconut oil, moisturizing balms, or moisturizing sprays for dogs, as well as moisturizing shampoos for dogs to help protect the hair and keep it in good condition. It is important to wet the dog's hair thoroughly before applying the product so that it penetrates effectively.
✔ To brush the dog's hair, it is recommended to start with the paws. Lift the hair upwards and brush in layers using a fine-tooth comb. If you encounter a knot, do not pull it with the comb as it could break the hair. Instead, gently untangle the knot with your fingers and then pass the comb through once it is completely undone. Avoid direct contact with the dog's skin and brush gently.
✔ Once you have finished brushing the dog's hair, it is recommended to check again for any knots. If you still find knots, untangle them with your fingers and comb through them again. Finally, it is advisable to comb the dog's coat to ensure there are no tangles.

Brushing Long-Haired Dogs:
✔ To brush a long-haired dog, it is recommended to start by using a flat brush and a flat comb to check for any knots. This helps locate the areas where the hair is most tangled and address them first.
✔ Next, it is advisable to use a moisturizing product that will help protect the hair and facilitate brushing. It is important to wet the dog's hair thoroughly before applying the product so that it penetrates effectively.
✔ To brush the dog's hair, it is recommended to start with the paws. Lift the hair upwards and brush in layers, using a flat brush. If you encounter a knot, do not pull on it with the brush, as it could break the hair. Instead, untangle the knot with your fingers and then brush again once it's completely undone. Avoid direct contact with the dog's skin and brush gently.
✔ The tail, which usually has the longest hair, should be brushed in layers. Apply a little moisturizing product to the hair and brush gently, being careful not to pull on the hair.
✔ Once you have finished brushing the dog's hair, it is recommended to check again for any knots. If you still find knots, untangle them with your fingers and then brush through them again. Finally, it is advisable to comb the dog's coat to ensure there are no tangles.

What to Do If the Dog Refuses:
If your dog refuses to be brushed, it may be because they are scared or not accustomed to this routine. Here are some tips to help acclimate your dog to brushing:
✔ Start brushing your dog when they are young so they get used to the routine.
✔ Conduct short and positive brushing sessions, rewarding your dog with treats and affection during and after brushing.
✔ Use a soft-bristle brush and gentle pressure when brushing their coat.

- If your dog is afraid of the brush, you can try having them touch the brush with their snout and reward them when they do it before moving on to longer brushing sessions.
- If your dog still refuses to be brushed, you can try offering them a distraction, such as a chew toy, while you brush them.
- If you have difficulty brushing your dog or have concerns about their health, consult a veterinarian for advice and recommendations.

In summary, grooming your dog's coat is essential to maintain their health and prevent knots and tangles. It's important to choose the right brush based on their hair length and regularly brush their coat using suitable products to facilitate grooming and protect the fur. If your dog refuses to be brushed, it's recommended to get them used to this routine from a young age and have short and positive brushing sessions, rewarding them with treats and affection. If you have concerns or difficulties with brushing, don't hesitate to consult a veterinarian for personalized advice.

How to Deal with Hair Loss?

There are several reasons why your dog may be losing their hair:

1. **Shedding:** All dogs shed to some extent, depending on their breed and age. Shedding is a normal process of renewing the fur and can result in temporary hair loss.
2. **Diet:** Inadequate nutrition can affect the quality of your dog's skin and coat, leading to hair loss. Ensure they receive quality food and an adequate amount of water.
3. **Parasites:** Parasites such as fleas and ticks can cause hair loss in your dog by irritating the skin. Use an anti-parasitic treatment to eliminate these parasites from your dog.
4. **Stress:** Stress can lead to hair loss in your dog. Try to reduce your dog's stress by providing them with plenty of exercise, playtime, and social interactions.
5. **Health Issues:** Some diseases or medical conditions can cause hair loss in your dog, such as allergies, skin infections, or hormonal disorders.

There are several ways to deal with dog hair loss and the "hair everywhere" situation in your home:

1. **Regularly Brush Your Dog:** Regularly brushing your dog can help remove dead hair and reduce the amount of hair that ends up in your home. Choose a brush that is suitable for your dog's breed and coat length. Pin brushes are often recommended for long-haired dogs, while wide-toothed brushes are better for short-haired dogs. Brushing them at least once a week can help reduce the amount of hair in your home.
2. **Use a Retractable Bristle Brush:** These brushes have bristles that retract when used, effectively removing dead hair from your dog's coat without leaving hair on your carpet or clothing. They are particularly useful for long-haired dogs that can shed a lot of hair.
3. **Use a Dog Hair Vacuum:** There are vacuums specifically designed to remove dog hair from your carpets, cushions, and other fabrics. These vacuums have filters that can capture dog hair and prevent it from ending up in the dust bag or container. Using a dog hair vacuum can be especially helpful for long-haired dogs or those that shed a lot of hair.
4. **Invest in Blankets and Cushions for Your Dog:** Using blankets and cushions that can be easily washed will allow you to keep your home clean without having to spend time cleaning up dog hair. You can use these blankets and cushions in the places where your dog is used to resting, such as their bed or cushion, to prevent hair from ending up on your carpets and cushions.
5. **Regularly Clean Your Home Surfaces:** Using a vacuum cleaner or a broom to remove dog hair from the surfaces of your home (such as carpets and cushions) can help reduce hair buildup. If you notice that certain

areas of your home are particularly prone to dog hair buildup, you can try cleaning them more often or using a dog hair vacuum to remove hair more easily. It is also important to regularly change the filters of your vacuum cleaner to maintain good performance and prevent dog hair from accumulating in the motor or hoses.

6. **Rubber Gloves:** If you have difficulty removing dog hair that is stuck to certain surfaces, you can try using a pair of rubber gloves to wipe away the hair. Rubber gloves have a rough surface that can help remove dog hair that is difficult to remove with a broom or vacuum cleaner.

It should be noted that hair loss can be a sign of health problems in your dog. If you notice excessive or sudden hair loss, it is recommended to consult a veterinarian to determine the cause and find appropriate treatment.

Give Your Dog a Bath.

Border Collies have a dense double coat, which means they can be more sensitive to water temperature and the use of bathing products. Make sure to use a gentle shampoo specially designed for dogs and avoid over-wetting their undercoat, as this can make drying more difficult. The frequency of baths may vary depending on your Border Collie's lifestyle, but in general, avoid bathing them too frequently to avoid disrupting the natural balance of their skin oils.

- ✔ You may not need to bathe your dog as often as you think. In general, a bath every two to three months is sufficient for most dogs. However, if they enjoy playing outside and getting dirty, you may need to bathe them more often.
- ✔ Use a dog shampoo that is suitable for their coat and skin. Do not use human products as they can be irritating to your dog's skin.
- ✔ Be sure to rinse your dog's shampoo thoroughly to avoid skin irritations. You can use a shower or a garden hose to rinse them, but make sure the water is not too hot.

Here's how to proceed:

1. Fill a bathtub or shower with warm (but not too hot) water and add a small amount of dog shampoo.
2. Place your dog in the water and gently massage the shampoo into their fur, starting with the back and working your way to the legs.
3. Be sure to rinse your dog's shampoo thoroughly to avoid skin irritations.
4. Dry your dog by patting them with a towel or using a hairdryer set to a low temperature.
5. Avoid getting your dog's head wet, as water and shampoo can get into their eyes and ears, causing irritation. Use a damp sponge to clean your dog's face if necessary.
6. Use a non-slip mat in the bathtub or shower to prevent your dog from slipping.
7. If your dog is nervous or anxious during the bath, speak to them in a calm and reassuring voice and reward them with dog treats.
8. If you are using a hairdryer, use it at a low temperature to avoid burning your dog's skin.
9. If your dog is very dirty or has skin issues, seek advice from your veterinarian before giving them a bath.

What to Do If Your Dog Refuses?

If your dog refuses to take a bath, they may be afraid of water or not accustomed to this routine. Here are some tips to help acclimate your dog to bath time:

1. Start giving baths to your dog when they are young so they become accustomed to this routine.

2. Keep baths short and positive, rewarding your dog with treats and affection during and after the bath.
3. Use lukewarm water and be sure not to put your dog's head underwater.
4. If your dog is afraid of water, you can try putting a bathing suit or a bathing coat on them to protect and comfort them during the bath.
5. If your dog still refuses to take a bath, you can try offering them a distraction, such as a chew toy, while you wash them.
6. If you have difficulty giving your dog a bath or have concerns about their health, consult a veterinarian for advice and recommendations.
7. Start by letting your dog smell the shampoo and the water without immersing them directly in the bathtub. This can help reduce their anxiety.
8. Reward your dog with treats and affection throughout the process to encourage and reinforce positive behavior.
9. Use a shallow bathtub or shower to make your dog feel safer and more comfortable.
10. Try to associate bath time with a pleasant activity for your dog, such as a walk or playtime.
11. If your dog is very reluctant, consult a dog trainer or a veterinarian for advice and assistance.

It's important never to force your dog to take a bath as this could worsen their anxiety and make the situation more challenging in the future.

Brushing Teeth

Dental problems are common in dogs, especially in older dogs. To prevent dental issues, brush your dog's teeth at least once a week using a toothbrush and toothpaste specially designed for dogs. You can also use dental sticks or chew bones to help clean your dog's teeth. If you notice dental problems such as decayed teeth or swollen gums, take your dog to the vet for treatment.

Here's how to do it:
- Buy a toothbrush and toothpaste specially designed for dogs. Do not use human toothpaste as it can be toxic to dogs.
- Place your dog on a stable and secure surface, such as a table or a dog grooming surface.
- Desensitize the dog to mouth handling by rewarding them with treats when they allow you to touch their muzzle.
- Progress by touching the dog's teeth and lifting their lips with your finger, then using a small fabric toothbrush to brush their teeth with flavored toothpaste.
- Gently open their mouth and place the toothbrush on their teeth. Use circular motions and gentle pressure to brush your dog's teeth and gums.
- Brush each tooth individually, making sure to clean all surfaces of the tooth, including the sides and the gumline.
- Once you have brushed all of your dog's teeth, rinse their mouth with water and give them a drink to help rinse their mouth.
- Don't forget to continue rewarding the dog with treats during tooth brushing to make them more comfortable.
- Gradually increase the duration and frequency of tooth brushing sessions, using a real toothbrush if necessary.
- Maintain a regular tooth brushing routine to maintain your dog's oral health.
- Start brushing their teeth when they are young so that they become accustomed to this routine.

What if the dog refuses?

If your dog refuses to have their teeth brushed, they may be scared or not accustomed to this routine. Here are some tips to help acclimate your dog to tooth brushing:

- Start brushing their teeth when they are young so that they become accustomed to this routine.
- Have short and positive tooth brushing sessions, rewarding your dog with treats and affection during and after brushing.
- Use a toothbrush and toothpaste specifically designed for dogs, and make sure not to apply too much pressure on your dog's teeth and gums.
- If your dog still refuses to have their teeth brushed, you can try giving them chew toys that help clean their teeth and reduce plaque. You can also try giving them kibble or food specially designed to help clean teeth.
- Start by getting your dog used to mouth handling by giving them treats and rewarding them when they allow you to touch their muzzle.
- Gradually introduce the toothbrush by first using a small fabric toothbrush to rub the teeth with flavored toothpaste, then moving on to a real toothbrush when your dog is more comfortable.
- Begin by brushing your dog's teeth for short periods and gradually increase the duration of each session.
- Always reward your dog with treats during and after teeth brushing to make them more comfortable.
- If your dog still refuses to allow teeth brushing, consult your veterinarian for additional advice and recommendations.

You should regularly brush your dog's teeth to maintain their oral health and prevent the formation of tartar and gum diseases. If they refuse to allow teeth brushing, it is recommended to find ways to get them accustomed to this routine and seek the assistance of a veterinarian if necessary.

He still smells bad even after a bath.

There are several reasons why a dog may still have a bad odor even after taking a bath. Here are some actions to take to address this issue:

1. **Check for an ear infection or skin irritation.** If your dog has an ear infection or skin irritation, they may smell bad even after a bath. Consult your veterinarian for appropriate treatment.
2. **Check the quality of the water and soap used.** If the water is too hot or the soap is too harsh, it can irritate your dog's skin and give them a bad odor. Use lukewarm water and a gentle soap for your dog's bath.
3. **Monitor your dog's diet.** Inadequate nutrition can affect the quality of your dog's skin and coat and result in a bad odor. Ensure they are receiving quality food and an adequate amount of water.
4. **Regularly brush your dog's coat.** Shedding and dead hair can lead to a bad odor if not removed regularly. Brush your dog at least once a week to eliminate dead hair and improve skin blood circulation.
5. **Use high-quality conditioner or after-shampoo** to help detangle the fur and leave it soft and shiny. This can help prevent the accumulation of dead hair and improve your dog's odor.
6. **Use a snowball scent spray** or similar products on their fur to mask unpleasant odors.
7. **Use essential oils like lavender**, tea tree, or rosemary on your dog's fur to mask unpleasant odors.
8. **Use aromatic massage brushes** that release essential oil when brushing your dog to mask unpleasant odors.

It should be noted that these measures will not address the underlying issue of your dog's bad odor and should not replace any necessary medical treatment. If you find that the bad odor persists despite these measures, it is recommended to consult a veterinarian for a proper diagnosis and treatment.

Trim the Nails.

Trimming the nails is also essential for Border Collies. However, this breed is generally very active and tends to naturally wear down their nails through physical activities. Make sure the nails do not become too long to prevent discomfort during walks or activities. Pay attention to the color of the nails: if they are clear, you can see the living part (blood vessels), but if they are dark, it may be more challenging to determine where to cut. In this case, exercise caution or seek professional help.

- You should first let them get used to the scissors and associate them with positive stimuli by allowing them to sniff them while rewarding them. This step should last for a few days
- If your dog doesn't walk much on hard surfaces, their claws can become too long. To prevent this from happening, regularly trim your dog's claws using nail clippers.
- Make sure to only cut the white part of the claws, as the pink part is filled with nerves and blood vessels. Cutting too close may cause your dog to bleed.

Trim your dog's claws:

1. Create a relaxed environment and get your dog accustomed to being touched and having their paws handled if you haven't done so already.
2. Ask another person to assist you by holding the dog.
3. Take one of the paws, examine the claws to locate the living tissue, and determine how far to trim.
4. Cut the claw using scissors for a quick and safe trim.
    - If you hear a "click" while trimming your dog's nails, it means you've reached the bone and should stop cutting.
    - If you cut more than necessary, remain calm and stop the bleeding with powder while soothing your dog.

What to do if the dog refuses?

If your dog refuses to have its nails trimmed, it may be scared or not accustomed to this routine. Here are some tips to help your dog get used to nail trimming:
- Start trimming their nails when they are young, so they get used to this routine.
- Make nail trimming sessions short and positive, rewarding your dog with treats and affection during and after the trim.
- Use an appropriate pair of nail clippers for dogs and make sure not to cut too close to the quick.
- You can try getting them to touch the clippers with their muzzle and reward them when they do it before moving on to longer trimming sessions.
- If your dog still refuses to let you trim its nails, you can try offering a distraction, such as a chew toy, while you trim its nails.

When to visit the veterinarian: If your dog is too fearful and even shows aggression during the sessions, it is recommended to consult a veterinarian or a canine groomer. Additionally, if your dog has black nails, it is advisable to seek the expertise of a specialist.

Massage for Your Dog

It should be noted that massage can be beneficial for dogs of all breeds and sizes, but it's important to respect your dog's limits and not force the massage if they are not comfortable. Here is a step-by-step guide on how to massage your dog:

- **Find a comfortable and quiet place for your dog.** Ensure that they feel safe and relaxed before starting the massage.
- **Be kind and gentle.** Use a soothing voice and slow movements to reassure your dog.
- **Start with the front legs.** Slide your hands along your dog's legs, using circular motions to relax the muscles.
- **Move on to the hind legs.** Use the same circular motions to massage your dog's thighs and hips.
- **Massage the back and shoulders.** Use your hands to follow the contours of your dog's back, taking care not to apply too much pressure on the bones.
- **Massage the chest and belly.** Slide your hands along your dog's chest, using gentle circular movements. Avoid massaging the belly too vigorously, as it can be uncomfortable for them.
- **Finish with the head and neck.** Use your fingers to massage the muscles of your dog's neck, being careful not to apply pressure to the eyes or ears. You can also scratch behind the ears to help them relax.

It's important to carefully monitor your dog's reactions during the massage and let them withdraw if they've had enough. If they appear relaxed and enjoy the massage, you can continue until they get up or move away. If they show signs of discomfort or stress, stop the massage immediately and allow them to rest.

Education and Training:

Training and educating your dog are essential to provide them with a happy and balanced life. This breed of dog is highly intelligent and capable of retaining many commands and executing them precisely, thanks to its excellent memory and concentration abilities. They also enjoy discovering new things and taking on new challenges, making them an exceptional animal to train and educate.

Basic Training:

Basic training consists of a set of fundamental behaviors and commands that dog owners should teach their dogs to enhance communication and the relationship between them. It typically includes commands such as "sit,"down,"stay,"come," and "walk on a leash." It may also include teaching appropriate social behaviors, such as not jumping on people or excessive barking. Basic training should begin at a young age, as it can help strengthen communication and create a solid foundation for learning more complex behaviors in the future. Basic training can be taught in various ways, including the use of rewards, positive reinforcement, and gentle correction.

Rules to Follow:

Here are some basic rules to know when training your dog:

1. **Be Consistent:** it's important to always use the same commands and training techniques so that he understands what you expect from him.
2. **Be Patient:** training a dog takes time and patience. Don't expect him to understand everything right away, and be prepared to repeat exercises several times before he masters them.
3. **Reward Good Behavior:** use treats, pets, and encouraging words to praise him when he successfully completes a task. This will encourage him to continue learning and behaving well.
4. **Ignore Undesirable Behaviors:** If he does something wrong, don't scold or punish him. Simply ignore the undesirable behavior and wait for him to do something good to reward him.
5. **Keep Training Sessions Short:** Dogs have limited attention spans, so it's important not to overwork them during training. Have short training sessions of a few minutes several times a day rather than long sessions once a week.
6. **Be Positive and Encouraging:** Dog training should be an enjoyable time for him. Use a gentle and encouraging tone of voice, and make training a fun experience for your dog.
7. **Be Persistent:** Dog training can sometimes be challenging, and it's normal to encounter obstacles. Don't lose hope and continue working with your dog until he understands what you expect from him.

Learning to Sit.

The "sit" command instructs your dog to place his bottom on the ground and remain still in that position until given a new command. This command can be useful in various situations, such as when you want him to wait before going through a door or when you need to give him a simple basic command to stay calm.

Step-by-Step Procedure for Teaching the "Sit" Command:
1. Start by choosing your keyword for this command, for example, "sit."
2. Sit down next to him and show him a reward.
3. Give your command using the keyword "sit" and wait for him to perform the requested action.

4. If he doesn't perform the action, you can help him by gently pushing his bottom until he sits down.
5. When he sits down, immediately give him the reward and praise him. Use an enthusiastic tone of voice and pet your dog to congratulate him.
6. Repeat the exercise several times until he understands the command.
7. Once he understands the command, you can start adding distractions and increasingly difficult situations to reinforce the learning. For example, you can ask him to sit when there are other people or animals nearby.

Learning to Lie Down.

The "lie down" command: this command instructs your dog to lie down on the floor and remain still in that position until he receives a new command.
- Start by choosing your keyword for this command, for example, "down."
- Sit down next to him and show him a reward.
- Give your command using the keyword "down" and wait for him to perform the requested action.
- If he doesn't perform the action, you can help him by gently pushing him onto his back until he lies down.
- When he lies down, immediately give him the reward and praise him. Use an enthusiastic tone of voice and pet your dog to praise him.
- Repeat the exercise several times until he understands the command.
- Once he understands the command, you can start adding distractions and increasingly difficult situations to reinforce the learning. For example, you can ask him to lie down when there are other people or animals around.

Learning to come.

The command "come": This command instructs your dog to come to you and stay by your side.

1. Start by choosing your keyword for this command, for example, "come".
2. Sit down next to him and show him a reward.
3. Give your command using the keyword "come" and wait for him to perform the requested action.
4. If he does not perform the action, you can help him by gently pulling the leash until he comes to you.
5. When he comes to you, immediately give him the reward and praise him. Use an enthusiastic tone of voice and pet him to show your appreciation.
6. Repeat the exercise several times until he understands the command.
7. Once he understands the command, you can start adding distractions and increasingly challenging situations to reinforce the learning. For example, you can ask him to come to you when there are other people or animals around.

Learning to stay.

The command "ne bouge pas" or "stay": this command instructs your dog to remain still in their current position until they receive a new command.

1. Start by choosing your keyword for this command, for example, "stay."
2. Sit next to your dog and show them a reward.
3. Give the command using the keyword "stay" and wait for them to perform the requested action.

4. If they don't perform the action, you can assist them by gently blocking them with your hand or holding them by the leash until they remain still.
5. Once he remains still, immediately give him the reward and praise him. Use an enthusiastic tone of voice and pet him to praise him.
6. Repeat the exercise several times until he understands the command.
7. Once he understands the command, you can begin adding distractions and progressively more challenging situations to reinforce the learning. For example, you can ask him to stay still when there are other people or animals nearby.

Learning to drop the object.

The command "give" or "drop": this command instructs your dog to release an object held in its mouth.
1. Start by choosing your keyword for this command, for example, "release."
2. Sit next to your dog and show him a reward.
3. Give your command using the keyword "give" and wait for him to perform the requested action.
4. If he does not perform the action, you can help by gently opening his mouth and removing the object from his mouth.
5. When he releases the object, immediately give him the reward and praise him. Use an enthusiastic tone of voice and pet him to praise him.
6. Repeat the exercise several times until he understands the command.
7. Once he understands the command, you can start adding distractions and increasingly difficult situations to reinforce the learning. For example, you can ask him to release an object when there are other people or animals around.

Learning not to bark.

The command "quiet": this command asks your dog to stop barking or making noise.
Start by choosing your keyword for this command, for example, "quiet." Or "shut."

1. Sit down next to him and show him a reward.
2. Give your command using the keyword "quiet" and wait for him to perform the requested action.
3. If he doesn't perform the action, you can help him by giving him a basic command like "stay" or "sit," which will ask him to calm down and stay still.
4. When he stops making noise, immediately give him the reward and praise him. Use an enthusiastic tone of voice and pet him to praise him.
5. Repeat the exercise several times until he understands the command.
6. Once he understands the command, you can begin to add distractions and increasingly difficult situations to reinforce the learning. For example, you can ask him to stay quiet when there are other people or animals around.

What to do if the dog refuses to obey?

There are several things you can try if he refuses to obey basic training commands:

- **Make sure he understands the command you are giving him.** Use simple words and repeat the command often until he understands.

- **Be patient and consistent in your training.** Don't give commands if you're not ready to enforce them.
- **Use rewards to encourage him to obey.** Offer him a treat or a pat whenever he obeys a command.
- **If he has trouble obeying a specific command,** try to show him what you expect from him. For example, if you ask him to sit and he doesn't understand, show him how to sit by doing it yourself.
- **Use a firm but calm tone of voice when giving him commands.** An authoritative tone of voice can help him understand that you are serious and that he must obey.
- **Keep training sessions short and frequent**. This can help him better remember commands and be more willing to follow them.
- **Be consistent in your training.** If you give a command and he doesn't obey it, don't reward him to avoid giving him the impression that he doesn't need to obey.
- **Use positive training techniques.** Instead of scolding or punishing your dog when he doesn't follow a command, encourage him by praising and rewarding him when he obeys.
- **If he has difficulty obeying a particular command,** try teaching him a similar command that is easier for him first. For example, if you ask him to lie down and he doesn't understand, try teaching him to sit first. Once he understands how to sit, you can then teach him how to lie down.
- **Ensure that he is well-fed and hydrated**. A dog that is hungry or thirsty may be less inclined to obey commands.
- **Make sure he gets enough exercise.** A bored or energy-filled dog may be less inclined to obey commands.
- **If he struggles to obey commands,** try teaching him to respond to verbal commands and hand signals. This can help him better understand what you expect from him.
- **If he struggles to obey commands in the presence of distractions,** try teaching him to obey in a calm, distraction-free environment. Once he understands how to obey in that environment, you can then teach him to obey in noisier or more animated situations.

Advanced Training.

Advanced dog training involves reinforcing the skills and behaviors acquired during basic dog training and learning new ones. This can include advanced commands such as "fetch,"retrieve,"drop it," as well as teaching behaviors like walking on a leash without pulling, socializing with other dogs and humans, and training for entertaining activities such as agility.

It is recommended to start advanced training for puppies when they are still young and provide them with plenty of rewards and positive reinforcement to encourage good behavior. It is also important to socialize them with other dogs and humans to build their confidence and emotional stability.

Learning to Fetch:

Teaching the "fetch" command: This involves hiding treats or toys and asking your dog to find them. You can use visual or verbal cues to help him understand what you expect from him.

Here is a detailed example of steps to teach your puppy the "fetch" command:

- Start with easy-to-find and unobtrusive objects. Choose a toy or treat that he likes and place it under a cushion or in an open drawer.

- Make sure he is looking at the object you are about to hide so he can remember what it looks like.

- Once you have hidden the object, say "fetch" to him in a cheerful and encouraging tone. You can also provide a visual cue by pointing to the place where you hid the object.

- Encourage him to search for the object by speaking to him gently and praising him when he finds it. If he has trouble finding the object, you can give him verbal cues by saying "it's over there" or "look under the cushion."

- Repeat this exercise several times with different objects and by hiding the object in increasingly challenging places. This will help him understand the "fetch" command and develop his ability to search for hidden objects.

- If he struggles to learn the "fetch" command or if he becomes frustrated or restless while playing this game, stop the exercise and try again later.

Learning to fetch:

Teaching the "fetch" command involves showing your puppy how to take an object with its mouth and bring it back to you. This can be useful for picking up toys or objects that your puppy has left around the house.

Here's a detailed example of steps to teach your dog to fetch:

- Choose a small, low-value object, such as a ball or a rubber toy, to start with. Make sure the object is clean and safe for your dog.

- Place the object in front of your dog and give the "fetch" command clearly and firmly. Use a tone of voice and gestures that indicate to your dog that you expect something from him.

- If he doesn't pick up the object, you can try showing him by picking it up with your mouth yourself or gently pushing it with your foot.

- Once he has picked up the object with his mouth, immediately reward him with a treat or a pet to reinforce the desired behavior.

- Repeat the exercise several times in a row using different objects and gradually increasing the difficulty. For example, you can use objects of different sizes and shapes, or hide them so that he has to search for them.

Learning to put down or deposit:

Teaching the "put" command: This involves showing your dog how to place an object in a specific location, such as a box or a basket. This can be useful for organizing his toys or teaching him to clean up his waste and put it in the trash.

Here is a detailed example of steps to teach your dog to put down or deposit an object:

- Choose a simple object that is the right size for your dog, such as a plush toy or a chew bone. Make sure the object is clean and safe for him.
- Place the object in an easily accessible location for him, such as on the floor or on a low table.
- Get his attention on the object by speaking to him gently or making a noise to make him look.
- Give the command "take" or "take this" by pointing at the object with your finger or making a hand gesture. Wait for him to take the object in his mouth.
- Once he has taken the object in his mouth, give the command "put" or "place" indicating where you want him to put the object, such as a box or a basket.
- If he doesn't understand the command, you can use positive reinforcement to help him understand what you expect from him. For example, you can give him a treat or verbal praise when he puts the object in the specified place.
- Repeat this exercise regularly, using different objects and moving the location where you want him to put the object. This will help him understand the "put" or "place" command and teach him to tidy up his toys or clean up his waste.

Learning the "fetch" command.:

While it's a classic game, fetching is a trick that doesn't come naturally to some dogs. It can be quite frustrating when they don't cooperate during playtime. Some dogs are not interested in the toy and won't even try; some will fetch the toy but won't bring it back, and then there are stubborn dogs who bring the toy back but won't let go. Here's how you can get started with this game with your dog:

1. Start by teaching the command "fetch" using a toy or treat as a reward. Show the object to the dog and say "fetch" while throwing it or placing it on the ground. Reward the dog every time it brings the object back to you.
2. Do reinforcement sessions by increasing the distance between you and the object you want the dog to fetch. Ask the dog to fetch the object while staying at a certain distance from you.
3. Vary the objects you want the dog to fetch. Use different toys and treats to keep their interest and reinforce learning.
4. Use distractions to reinforce learning. Add noises, movements, and people around you when you ask your dog to fetch the object. This will help strengthen their ability to focus on your command even in the presence of distractions.

5. Be patient and persistent. Learning a new command may take time, but by being consistent and rewarding them for their efforts, you will help them understand and respond quickly.

Learning to tidy up toys

You can teach your dog to tidy up their toys on command. This can be a useful skill to have them put away their toys when they're done playing, but it can also be a fun way to stimulate their brain. Here's how you can teach them:

- Choose a quiet and distraction-free place to start training.
- Start by encouraging them to pick up a toy and put it in their toy box by placing a treat near the box and asking them to "tidy up." Reward them each time they successfully put away a toy.
- Once they are comfortable with the idea of tidying up their toys, begin showing them how to put away multiple toys at once by placing a treat near the box and asking them to "tidy up."
- Reward them each time they correctly tidy up their toys, and repeat the exercise several times until they understand what is expected of them.
- Once they understand the command to tidy up their toys, you can start asking them to do so without a treat and teach them a specific command word like "tidy up" or "put away your toys."

It is advisable to remain patient and not force your dog to tidy up their toys if they do not immediately understand what is expected of them.

If they refuse to obey ?

If they are having difficulty learning to tidy up their toys, here are some additional tips:
1. Make sure they have an appropriately sized and accessible toy box. If the box is too small or placed in a hard-to-reach location, they may be less inclined to tidy up their toys.
2. Make sure the toy box is enticing for them. You can place treats or your dog's favorite toys in the box to encourage them to tidy up their toys.
3. Be consistent in your use of the tidying command. Always use the same command and reward them every time they tidy up their toys correctly.

It is also important to remember never to force your dog to tidy up their toys if they do not want to and to respect their boundaries. If they do not enjoy tidying up their toys, they may prefer other positive reinforcement activities or mental stimulation.

Learning to Recognize Objects

You can teach your dog to recognize different objects on command. This can be a useful skill to enable them to find specific objects when asked, but it can also be a fun way to stimulate their brain. Here's how you can teach them:
1. Choose a quiet and distraction-free place to start training.
2. Begin by showing your dog an object and giving it a name. For example, if you show them a ball, you can say "ball." Reward your dog every time they look at the object and repeat this exercise with different objects.
3. Once your dog is comfortable with the idea of recognizing different objects, start showing them the object and asking them to touch it with their paw or to find it. Reward them each time they correctly identify the object, and repeat the exercise several times until they understand what you expect from them.

4. Once they have learned how to recognize different objects, you can start teaching them specific commands for each object, such as "fetch the ball" or "touch the stuffed animal."

Learning Left and Right

It's essential to be able to communicate with your dog clearly and precisely, and teaching them to understand the words "left" and "right" can be useful in many situations. Here's how you can teach them to understand these words:

1. Choose a quiet and distraction-free location to start training.
2. Hold a treat in each hand and ask your dog to choose between the two by saying "left" or "right." Reward them with the treat from the hand they choose.
3. Repeat this exercise several times until they understand the words "left" and "right." You can also use gestures or pointing to indicate the direction to follow.
4. Once they understand the words "left" and "right," you can use them in other contexts to ask them to move in a specific direction. For example, you can ask them to turn left or right during leash walks or to move to the left or right when playing ball or frisbee games.
5. It is recommended to continue rewarding your dog every time they perform a correct action and not to punish them if they do not immediately understand what you expect from them.
6. It is also important to remember to always use the words "left" and "right" consistently and not use them in other contexts. This will help your dog quickly understand their meaning and use them correctly.

Learning to open and close the door?

You can teach your dog to open and close the door on command. This can be a useful skill for them to help you open and close the door when needed, but it can also be a fun way to stimulate their brain. Here's how you can teach them this exercise:

1. Choose a door with an easy-to-grasp handle for your dog and place a reward near the handle to encourage them to touch it.
2. When they touch the door handle, reward them and repeat this exercise several times until they understand what you expect from them.
3. Once they understand how to touch the door handle, begin to show them how to open the door by doing it yourself and giving them a reward each time they successfully open the door.
4. Repeat this exercise several times until they understand how to open the door on command.
5. Once they understand how to open the door, you can teach them how to close it using the same steps.

Positive Reinforcement Training:

To effectively educate and train your dog, it is important to use positive training methods, which involve rewarding good behavior and ignoring undesirable behavior. You can use treats, affection, or words of approval to reward them when they behave well and ignore or redirect their attention when they behave undesirably.

Rules to Follow:

1. **Choose rewards that motivate your dog:** You will use treats to reward them every time they sit on command.
2. **Use positive reinforcement markers:** You will use the word "good" as a positive reinforcement marker every time they sit on command.
3. **Pay attention to your body language and tone of voice:** You will maintain a calm and positive body language and speak in a soft and pleasant tone during training.
4. **Start with short and simple training sessions:** You will begin with training sessions of a few minutes each day and gradually increase the duration as they progress.
5. **Be patient and persistent:** You will be patient and repeat the exercises regularly until they master the skill of sitting on command.

An example of how to do it:

- Give your dog a treat and say "sit" while pointing to the floor.
- When he sits, give him a positive reinforcement marker ("good") and a treat.
- Repeat this exercise several times during the training session, rewarding him each time he sits on command.
- As he progresses, you can increase the difficulty by waiting longer before rewarding him when he sits on command or by giving him the "sit" command at random times instead of pointing to the floor.

The list of exercises:

Here are some practical examples of positive training exercises you can try with your dog while applying the same rules:

- **Sit:** Ask your dog to sit and reward him when he does. You can use a command word like "sit" or a hand gesture to indicate what you expect from him.
- **Down:** Ask him to lie down and reward him when he does. You can use a command word like "down" or a hand gesture to indicate what you expect from him.
- **Leash Walking:** Teach him to walk calmly on a leash using rewards to reinforce desired behaviors. If he pulls on the leash, stop and wait for him to calm down before resuming the walk.
- **Recall:** Teach him to come to you when called using rewards to reinforce the desired behavior. Use a command word like "here" or "come" and reward him every time he comes to you.
- **Wait:** Teach him to wait before eating or going through a door using a command word like "wait" and rewarding the desired behavior. This exercise can be helpful in preventing him from rushing to his food or going through a door without your permission.
- **Backing Up:** Ask him to walk backward using a hand gesture or a command word like "back up." Reward him when he consistently performs the exercise.
- **Turn Right and Left:** Ask him to turn right or left using a hand gesture or a command word like "turn right" or "turn left." Reward him when he consistently performs the exercise.

- **Jump Over an Obstacle:** Teach him to jump over an obstacle using a hand gesture or a command word like "jump" or "over." You can use a stick or a bar to set the obstacle. Reward him when he consistently performs the exercise.
- **Fetch an Object:** Teach him to pick up and bring an object using a hand gesture or a command word like "take" or "fetch." You can use a toy or a ball as the object. Reward him when he consistently performs the exercise.
- **Stay calm:** Teach him to stay calm and relax when excited or stressed using a command word like "calm" or "relax." Reward him when he manages to calm down and relax.
- **Find:** Teach your pet to find a hidden object using a command word like "find" or "search." You can hide a toy or a treat and reward him when he finds the object.
- **Walk beside you without pulling on the leash:** Teach him to walk beside you without pulling on the leash using rewards to reinforce the desired behavior. If he pulls on the leash, stop and wait for him to calm down before resuming the walk.
- **Pass through doors and stairs in a controlled manner:** Teach him to pass through doors and stairs in a controlled manner using a command word like "wait" or "slowly" and rewarding the desired behavior. This exercise can be useful to prevent rushing into dangerous places or disturbing other individuals.
- **Greet guests in a controlled manner:** Teach him to greet guests in a controlled manner using a command word like "hello" or "hi" and rewarding the desired behavior. This exercise can be useful to prevent your dog from jumping on or disturbing guests.
- **Ignore distractions:** Teach him to ignore distractions such as passersby, animals, or loud noises using a command word like "leave" or "ignore" and rewarding the desired behavior. This exercise can be useful to help him stay focused in public or in environments with many distractions.
- **Close the door:** Teach him to close a door using a hand gesture or a command word like "close" and reward the desired behavior. This exercise can be useful to prevent your dog from going out through an open door or disturbing other individuals.
- **Drop an object:** Teach him to drop an object using a hand gesture or a command word like "release" and reward the desired behavior. This exercise can be useful to prevent your dog from chewing or destroying unwanted items.
- **Stay alone:** Teach him to stay alone using a command word like "stay" and reward the desired behavior. This exercise can be useful to help him feel comfortable when left alone at home.

- **Do not jump on people:** Teach him not to jump on people using a command word like "down" or "no jump" and reward the desired behavior. This exercise can be useful to prevent your dog from jumping on visitors or disturbing other individuals.
- **Do not escape:** Teach him not to escape using a command word like "stay" or "don't go" and reward the desired behavior. This exercise can be useful to prevent your dog from escaping your yard or house.

What to do if he doesn't obey?

It can be frustrating when a dog doesn't respond to commands or doesn't seem to react to positive training. Here are a few steps you can take if he doesn't obey commands or respond to positive training:

1. **Ensure you understand your dog's needs:** First and foremost, it's important to understand your dog's needs and ensure you provide enough exercise, social interaction, and mental stimulation. If lacking in these essential elements, it can be challenging for him to concentrate and respond to commands.

2. **Be clear and consistent in your requests:** Ensure you communicate your requests to your dog clearly and consistently. Use simple words and gestures, repeating them regularly to help him understand what you expect.

3. **Use positive reinforcement:** Consistently reward him when he obeys commands. Use rewards like treats, petting, or praise words to reinforce desired behaviors. This can help strengthen the positive association between commands and rewards and encourage voluntary obedience.

4. **Train regularly:** Regular training can help strengthen communication and the bond between you and your dog. Try to dedicate time every day to training and teaching new commands and behaviors.

It's important to note that obedience and positive training can be complex processes and each dog is different. If he fails to sit on command, do not reprimand or punish him. Instead, simply restart the exercise and reward your dog when he succeeds. Keep repeating this exercise regularly during your training until he masters the skill of sitting on command.

Remember, training a dog can take time and require patience. Don't expect him to master every new skill immediately and be prepared to repeat exercises multiple times until he fully understands what you expect from him. By using positive training methods and maintaining a calm, patient attitude, you can help him learn new skills effectively and enjoyably for both of you.

The Use of Clicker Training.

This method uses a "clicker" (a small device that makes a "click" sound when pressed) to reinforce the desired behavior. The clicker is associated with a reward, such as a treat, and is used to mark the desired behavior at the moment it occurs.

The clicker is a tool that has been used for many years in the United States for animal training. It was used by the military to train dolphins for certain missions, such as trapping enemy ships. The use of clicker training for canine education is more recent and increasingly popular in North America and elsewhere in the world. The method involves reinforcing the positive behaviors of the animal and has proven to be quite effective.

- **Advantages:** This method is often considered a gentle and effective way to learn specific behaviors.
- **Disadvantages:** This method can be complex and may require training to be used correctly.

Here are the general steps to use the clicker training method to educate a dog:

1. Start by introducing the clicker to your dog and associate it with a reward, such as a treat. You can do this by simply making a "click" each time you give your dog a treat and repeating this association several times until they understand that the "click" means they will receive a reward.

2. Once they've understood the association between the "click" and the reward, you can begin using the clicker to mark the desired behavior. For example, if you want them to sit, wait for them to sit on their own and make a "click" immediately followed by a reward. Repeat this step several times until they understand that the action of sitting is reinforced by the "click" and the reward.

3. Once they've understood the desired behavior, you can start using a verbal cue (e.g., "sit") to ask them to sit. Give the verbal cue before they sit and make a "click" and reward when they do. Repeat this step several times until they understand that the verbal cue means they should sit to receive a reward.

4. Once they've understood the desired behavior and respond well to the verbal cue, you can begin reducing the frequency of rewards. For instance, you can reward every two or three times initially, then every five or six times, and gradually less often until you no longer need to reward every time. This is called gradual extinction and allows your dog to continue performing the desired behavior even if they don't always receive a reward.

Here are some concrete examples of using the clicker training method:

1. **Teaching a dog to sit:** You can start by placing a treat near its nose and slowly moving it towards the back of the dog's head. When it naturally sits to follow the treat, the trainer presses the clicker and gives the treat to the dog.

2. **Teaching a dog to come when called:** You can start by clicking each time the dog comes towards you, even if it doesn't respond to a specific call. Then, you can begin to call its name and click each time it comes when called.

In general, clicker training can be a useful tool for dog education and training, especially for teaching specific and complex behaviors. However, like any method of education and training, you should choose the one that best suits your dog and your goals.

Classical Conditioning

Have you ever thought your puppy had a sixth sense? Somehow knowing without seeing that a favorite human is approaching the front door? It's not ESP, it's classical conditioning. They hear, smell, and react to signals too subtle for our human senses.

Classical conditioning refers to a learning process where learning occurs by association. You condition your dog's innate reflexes to respond to subtle cues. Over time, your dog learns to associate the cue with the event. Mastering the concept of classical conditioning will help you understand how your dog comprehends, relates, and interprets information. This form of learning is also known as Pavlovian or associative learning. Ivan Pavlov was a Russian physiologist who discovered that dogs would automatically salivate when presented with food. He trained his dogs to associate the sound of a bell with the presentation of food, eventually succeeding in making the dogs salivate with just the sound of a bell.

Pavlov's Principles of Classical Conditioning.

Classical conditioning is learned through association and was first demonstrated by Ivan Pavlov.
Pavlov showed that dogs could be conditioned to salivate at the sound of a bell if that sound was repeatedly presented alongside giving them food. The dogs initially received the food, they salivated. The food was the **unconditioned stimulus**, and salivation was an **unconditioned response (innate)**.

Then, Pavlov rang the bell **(neutral stimulus)** before giving the food.
After several pairings, the dogs would salivate when they heard the bell even when no food was given. The bell had become **the conditioned stimulus**, and the salivation had become the conditioned response.
The dogs had **learned** to associate the bell with food, and the sound of the bell triggered salivation.
Pavlov demonstrated that classical conditioning leads to learning through association.

- ✔ The **unconditioned response** was the dogs' natural salivation in response to seeing or smelling their food.
- ✔ The **unconditioned stimulus** was the sight or smell of the food itself.
- ✔ The **conditioned stimulus** was the sound of the bell, which previously had no association with food.
- ✔ The **conditioned response** was hence the dogs' salivation in response to the bell ringing, even in the absence of food.

EXAMPLES
You may have unknowingly applied the principles of classical conditioning to your dog. If your dog enjoys walks and associates the sound of its leash being taken from its spot with an imminent walk, does it get excited just hearing the leash? That's classical conditioning at work.

A less amusing example might be your dog's reaction at the vet's office. Under normal circumstances, it might be okay with strangers handling it. But unpleasant memories from prior vet visits can make it associate the vet with stress and discomfort, leading to unusual fear or aggression.

Another common example happens when new puppy owners start leash-walking their pup. When they encounter another dog, the new pet parent instinctively tenses up and holds the leash tightly when meeting another dog. It's understandable. It's an instinctive response. But the unintended outcome might be that your dog mirrors your tense and protective behavior every time it sees another dog during a walk.

IN A NUTSHELL

The legendary animal behaviorist Bob Bailey, whose credits include directing marine mammal training for the U.S. Navy program, explains classical conditioning this way: your dog develops a positive, negative, or neutral association with all surrounding stimuli. In simple terms, every moment counts when you're training your dog.

Mental Stimulation Exercise.

Dogs need plenty of exercise and mental stimulation to stay happy and healthy. To help manage mood swings and excessive barking, you can provide daily walks, games and physical activities, and offer interactive toys along with mental training exercises.

- **Daily Walk:** Offer your dog a daily walk of 30 to 60 minutes to allow it to expend energy and explore new territories.

Example:
1. Choose a 30 to 60-minute walking route.
2. Attach his leash and start walking.
3. Encourage your dog to safely explore and sniff around.

- **Ball Games:** Provide your dog with a ball game for entertainment and physical exercise. You can play ball with him or teach him to catch the ball with his front paws.

Example:
- Buy one or more rubber balls suitable for dogs.
- Show him how to play with the ball by throwing it and encouraging him to bring it back.
- You can also teach him to catch the ball with his front paws by showing him how and praising him each time he succeeds.

- **Agility Games:** Invest in an agility course or create one yourself using household items. This will help your dog work on coordination and determination while having fun.

Example:
1. Invest in an agility course or create one yourself using household items (such as cushions, bars, and plastic pipes).
2. Show your dog how to navigate the obstacles and encourage him to follow your lead.
3. Praise him every time he succeeds and repeat the exercise several times to enhance his coordination and determination.

- **Detective Games:** Hide treats around your house or garden and let your dog search for them. This will work on his hunting instinct and stimulate curiosity.

Example:
1. Choose one or more treats to hide around your house or garden.
2. Attach your dog's leash and let him sniff around to find the hidden treats.
3. Encourage him to search and find the treats by praising him each time he succeeds.

- **Learning new tricks:** Teach him new tricks to enhance his mind and strengthen your bond. For instance, you can teach him to pick up toys or stand on his hind legs.

Example:

1. Choose a trick to teach your dog (for example, "pick up toys").
2. Show him how to pick up a toy by taking it in his mouth and demonstrating it to him.
3. Encourage him to pick up the toy by praising him each time he succeeds and repeat the exercise several times until he understands the trick.

- **Obedience training:** Enroll your dog in an obedience class to teach him new skills and strengthen your bond.

Example:
1. Look for a dog training club or instructor in your area.
2. Enroll him in an obedience class and follow the instructor's guidance to teach new skills to your dog.

- **Puzzle games:** Provide your dog with puzzle games to stimulate its mind and help develop its logic and thinking.

Example:
1. Purchase a puzzle game designed for dogs (such as a tracking or moving pieces game).
2. Show your dog how to solve the puzzle by indicating the steps to follow and praising it each time it succeeds.

- **Dog work course:** Enroll your dog in a dog work course to teach it new skills and give it a mission to accomplish.

Example:
1. Look for a dog training club or instructor in your area.
2. Enroll your dog in a dog work course and follow the instructor's instructions to teach your dog new skills.

- **Nature walks:** Take him on hikes or walks in the woods to discover new landscapes and get some physical exercise.

Example:
- Choose a hiking or woodland walking route suitable for your dog.
- Attach his leash and start walking.
- Encourage him to explore and sniff safely while admiring the surrounding scenery.

- **Dog acting classes:** Enroll him in a dog acting class to teach him new skills and give him a chance to perform on stage.

Example:
1. Look for a canine drama club or instructor in your area.
2. Sign him up for a canine acting class and follow the instructor's instructions to teach him new skills.
3. Encourage your dog to express himself creatively and perform on stage.

- **Dog dance class:** Enroll him in a dog dance class to teach him new skills and give him the opportunity to express himself creatively.
Example:
1. Look for a dog dance club or instructor in your area.

2. Sign him up for a dog dance class and follow the instructor's instructions to teach him new skills.
3. Encourage your dog to express himself creatively and dance to music.

- **Visits to the dog park:** Take him to the dog park so he can meet other dogs and get some physical exercise.

Example:
1. Look for a dog park in your area.
2. Attach his leash and take him to the dog park.
3. Encourage him to play with other dogs and get some physical exercise while staying safe.

- **Swimming lessons:** Enroll him in a swimming class to teach him to swim and get physical exercise in the water.

Example:
1. Look for a dog swimming club or instructor in your area.
2. Sign him up for a swimming class and follow the instructor's instructions to teach your dog to swim and exercise in the water.

- **Card games:** Give your dog dog-friendly card games to stimulate his mind and teach him to solve puzzles.

Example:
- Buy a dog-friendly card game (e.g. a memory game or a coin-operated game).
- Show him how to solve the puzzles, pointing out the steps to follow and praising him every time he succeeds.

Mantrailig or tracking is an activity that involves following a human trail using the sense of smell. It can be used as a leisure activity for dogs and their owners, or as a search and rescue technique. The dog is trained to follow a specific scent trail, usually using a piece of personal item from the person to be found, such as clothing or an accessory. The dog must follow the trail until it finds the target person, then inform its handler of its discovery by barking or performing another previously taught action.

It's a good idea to keep your dog's safety in mind at all times, and not to push him to do exercises that might be too difficult or dangerous for him. You should also ensure that your dog has a healthy, balanced diet to support his need for exercise and mental stimulation.

Respect your dog's boundaries.

This dog breed is known for its energy and affection towards its owners. It is important to teach him to respect the limits of his territory and not to jump on people or bite them. You can use positive training methods to teach him to behave appropriately in society and respect the boundaries of his territory.

- ⊘ **Be consistent and patient:** Educating and training your dog can sometimes take time and require patience. You must be consistent and provide enough encouragement and rewards to help him learn new habits and behave appropriately.
- ⊘ **Show firmness and leadership:** Despite his loyalty and protective instinct, you need to show him that you are the pack leader and set clear boundaries. This will allow him to understand who is in charge and how to behave appropriately.
- ⊘ **Start early:** It is recommended to start your dog's education and training as early as possible, starting at 8 weeks of age. The earlier you start, the easier it will be for him to learn new things and develop good habits.
- ⊘ **Keep training sessions short and frequent:** short training sessions are more effective for dogs than longer, less frequent sessions. Try to do 10-15 minute training sessions several times a day rather than a single 30+ minute session.

V

Get to know your dog and understand his needs and limits. For example, some dogs need more exercise than others, and some may be more sensitive to certain stimuli.
- ➢ Take the time to play with your dog and exercise with him every day. This will help you better understand his physical and mental needs in terms of energy expenditure.
- ➢ Observe your dog when he interacts with other people or animals. This will help you identify situations that make him uncomfortable and avoid them.

Be patient and do not force your dog to do something that makes him uncomfortable. For example, don't force him to go near something that scares him or interact with people or animals he doesn't like.
- ➢ If he seems nervous or scared when you try to introduce him to new people or animals, don't force him to interact. Allow him to walk away and try again later when he feels more comfortable.
- ➢ If he does not like to be touched on certain parts of his body, respect his choice and do not touch him that way.

Use positive training and reinforce desired behaviors rather than punishing your dog for unwanted behaviors.
- ➢ Use rewards and praise to reinforce the behaviors you want to see in your dog, such as coming when called or sitting on command.
- ➢ Be careful not to unintentionally reinforce unwanted behaviors.For example, if he jumps on people in search of petting, don't pet him until he has calmed down.

Do not yell or hit your dog to punish him. These methods of correction are not effective and may even cause more serious behavioral problems in the long run.
- ➢ If he does something wrong, ignore it instead of yelling or hitting him.This will show him that the behavior is not acceptable without physically punishing him.
- ➢ If you need to interrupt unwanted behavior, use a firm voice and a physical signal, such as a whistle or hand gesture, to get your dog's attention.

Provide your dog with enough exercise and mental stimulation to keep him happy and healthy

- ➤ Make sure he gets enough exercise every day by taking him for walks and offering toys and activities to stimulate his mind.
- ➤ If you are away for the entire day, hire a dog walker or have a friend watch your dog to provide exercise and mental stimulation while you are away.

Keep your dog safe by putting him on a leash when he's off your property and providing a secure enclosure when he's inside.

- ➤ When you take your dog off your property, be sure to keep him on a leash to protect him and others.
- ➤ If you can't keep an eye on him at all times when he's indoors, offer him a secure enclosure or a room inside your home where he can be safe.

By following these tips, you can be sure of respecting your dog's limits and offering him a happy, fulfilling life. Don't forget that it's important to continue learning about your dog and adapting to his needs and limits over time.

Learning to live in society.

It's crucial to socialize your dog from an early age so that he learns to live in society peacefully and pleasantly. Here are a few tips on how to achieve this:

- Ensure that he gets enough exercise and entertainment to prevent boredom and restlessness.
- Teach your dog basic commands like "sit,"lie down," and "stay" to establish yourself as the pack leader and to teach him to calm down.
- Use positive reinforcement to strengthen your dog's desirable behaviors and show him that he can receive rewards when he behaves appropriately.
- Avoid putting your dog in stressful or confrontational situations, such as leaving him alone with unfamiliar dogs or exposing him to food or toys that could lead to fights.
- If he tends to be aggressive toward other dogs, avoid leaving him alone with them and make sure you always have control of the situation using a leash and harness.
- Ensure that he regularly meets other dogs and people to allow him to develop good social skills.
- Start socializing your dog from a young age, when he is still in the phase of social and emotional development. This will help him develop good social skills and better manage stressful social situations.
- Ensure that he regularly meets other dogs and people in controlled situations, such as on leash walks or visits to friends and family.
- If he tends to be shy or timid in the presence of other dogs or people, gradually expose him to these situations and give him time to adjust to these new experiences.

In summary, teaching your dog to live in society requires time and patience. By following these tips and working with a professional, you can help him develop good social skills and better manage stressful social situations.

Teaching Your Dog Proper Hygiene.

It is crucial to teach proper hygiene to your dog for several reasons. Firstly, it allows you to maintain a clean and odor-free home. Secondly, it can help prevent accidents and damage caused by him to your home. Additionally, learning proper hygiene can be beneficial for your dog's health as it helps prevent urinary tract infections and other health problems related to poor hygiene habits.

Here are some tips that can help you teach proper hygiene to your dog:

- Start training your dog from a young age when he is still in the developmental phase and has greater attention span.
- Choose a specific spot in your yard or home for him to do his business and ensure he goes there consistently. This will help him understand that this spot is designated for this purpose.
- Take your dog out regularly, especially after he has eaten or drunk, and when he has finished playing or sleeping. This will give him the opportunity to relieve himself regularly.
- Encourage him to do his business by rewarding him with treats or affection when he does so in the designated area.
- If he has an accident indoors, clean the area thoroughly to remove any scent traces, so he is not tempted to repeat the behavior.
- If you notice he starts to eliminate indoors, immediately take him outside so he can finish in the right place. Being attentive and patient can help him become house-trained and follow your home's hygiene rules.
- If he struggles with learning cleanliness or has regular accidents, do not hesitate to consult a veterinarian or an animal behaviorist for assistance. They can help you identify the causes of these behaviors and implement management strategies tailored to your needs.

In summary, teaching a dog cleanliness requires patience and perseverance. By following these tips and working with a professional, you should be able to help him understand how to eliminate properly.

Learning Not to Bark.

Here are some tips that can help you teach your dog not to bark:

- Identify the cause of his barking. Does he bark when he's hungry, thirsty, needs to go out, bored, stressed, or excited? Understanding the reason behind his barking will help you implement strategies to manage this behavior appropriately.
- Ensure he receives enough exercise and entertainment to prevent boredom and restlessness.
- Teach him basic commands like "sit,"lie down," and "stay," which will help him manage stressful situations better and calm down when exposed to stimuli that trigger his barking.
- Use positive reinforcement to reinforce your dog's desirable behaviors and show him that he can receive rewards when he behaves appropriately.
- If he barks repeatedly, use a firm and immediate "stop" or "no" to show him that this barking is not acceptable.
- If he barks when he's bored, give him chew toys or interactive toys, like a ball or a Kong, to help him channel his energy.

In summary, teaching your dog not to bark may take time and patience, but by following these tips, you can help him understand and manage his barking appropriately.

Learning Not to Nibble.

It's normal for him to nibble, especially if he's still a puppy and exploring his environment in this way. However, it's necessary to teach him not to nibble, as it can be dangerous for people and animals around him and can lead to undesirable behaviors such as aggression. Here are some steps you can follow to teach your dog not to nibble:

1. **Ignore the nibbling behavior.** If he nibbles, completely ignore him. Don't reward him with attention or play, even if he looks like he's begging you. If you respond to his demands, you're teaching him that it works, and he will continue to do it.
2. **Redirect his attention to appropriate toys.** If he nibbles, give him an appropriate toy to nibble on. Encourage him to play with the toy by praising him and giving him treats every time he nibbles on it.
3. **Teach him a "no" or "stop" command.** Use the "no" or "stop" command every time he starts nibbling. Reward him every time he obeys this command.
4. **Monitor your dog and intervene promptly.** If he starts nibbling, intervene quickly by using the "no" or "stop" command and redirecting him to an appropriate toy. The faster you intervene, the easier it will be for him to understand what you expect from him.
5. It's worth noting that aggressive nibbling can be a sign of stress or frustration in your dog. Make sure to provide him with enough exercise and mental stimulation and offer him a safe and stable environment. If he struggles to control his nibbling behaviors, providing him with chew toys or bones can help him expend his energy appropriately.
6. It may take time for him to stop nibbling, but with patience and diligence, you can teach him this good habit.

Here are some examples of how you could teach your dog a "no" or "stop" command:

1. **Choose a word or phrase that you will use as a command.** You can use "no" or "stop," or any other word or phrase that seems appropriate to you. The important thing is to choose a word or phrase that you consistently use whenever you want him to stop doing something.
2. **Use the command firmly and consistently.** Whenever he starts doing something you want him to stop, use the command firmly and consistently. For example, if he jumps on people, use the command "no" or "stop" every time he starts jumping and redirect him to an appropriate activity.
3. **Reward your dog every time he obeys the command.** Whenever he stops doing something you want him to stop in response to your command, reward him with a treat or positive attention. This will teach him that there are benefits to obeying your command.
4. **Be patient and consistent.** Teaching him a "no" or "stop" command may take time and patience. Be consistent in your use of the command and reward your dog every time he obeys to encourage him to continue doing so.

By using these steps consistently, you should be able to effectively teach your dog a "no" or "stop" command.

Teaching to Go to the Basket.

To teach your dog to go to the basket, you can follow these steps:

- ➤ Choose a comfortable and accessible basket for him. Place it in an area of your house where he often spends time.
- ➤ Start using the word "basket" every time he enters his basket. You can also use a hand gesture or a click to reinforce this signal.
- ➤ Reward your dog every time he voluntarily enters his basket. You can use treats, pets, or words of encouragement to reward him.
- ➤ Once he understands the concept of "basket," start using the phrase "go to the basket" to ask him to go there. Use the gesture or click to reinforce the signal.
- ➤ Reward your dog every time he goes to the basket on command. Continue to repeat the exercise until he reliably goes there when you ask him to.

Take the necessary time for him to fully understand the command and reward him each time he succeeds in going there on command.

If he refuses to obey?

If he refuses to go to the basket on command, here are some tips you can follow:

1. Make sure he fully understands the command. Use clear and simple words, and use the same signal (word, gesture, click) each time you ask him to go to the basket.
2. Make sure he has access to the basket at all times and that it is comfortable and accessible. If he doesn't want to go to the basket, it could be due to a comfort or accessibility issue.
3. Be patient and don't forget to reward him every time he goes there on command, even if it takes him a little while to get there. This will encourage him to repeat the desired behavior.
4. If he continues to refuse to go to the basket, there may be a health or pain issue preventing him from moving easily. In this case, it is necessary to consult a veterinarian to assess the situation.

Learning to Walk on a Leash?

Teaching your dog to walk on a leash can be an easy process if you follow the right steps. Here's how to proceed:

- **Choose an appropriate leash and collar for your dog.** Make sure the leash is long enough for him to move freely but not too long for him to escape or get tangled in objects. Use a nylon or leather collar rather than a harness, as it will make it easier to communicate your commands.
- **Start with short leash walks**. Attach the leash to your dog and walk in your yard or a quiet area to allow him to get used to the feeling of the leash.
- **Encourage your dog to walk by your side.** Use a treat or a toy to encourage him to walk close to you. If he pulls on the leash, stop and wait for him to calm down before resuming the walk.
- **Ensure he walks by your side without distraction.** Once he walks well on a leash in a calm environment, try walking him in busier places to help him get used to distractions.
- **Reward your dog every time he walks on the leash calmly and obediently.** This will encourage him to repeat the desired behavior.

You must take the necessary time for him to get used to walking on a leash and not leave him on a leash alone before he is ready.

If he refuses to obey?

If he refuses to obey your commands when walking on a leash, here are some tips you can follow:

1. Make sure he understands the command. Use clear and simple words, and use the same signal (word, gesture, click) each time you ask him to walk on a leash.
2. Check that he has been trained effectively to obey this command. If he has not been trained to walk on a leash effectively, he may not understand what you expect from him.
3. Be patient and remember to reward your dog every time he walks on a leash calmly and obediently. This will encourage him to repeat the desired behavior.

4. If he continues to refuse to obey, there may be a health problem or pain that prevents him from moving easily. In this case, it is necessary to consult a veterinarian to assess the situation.

Walking Your Dog Without a Leash

It is recommended to always walk your dog on a leash when you are outside your property, except in areas where dogs are allowed to be off-leash. The leash helps to protect him and others. However, it is possible to walk him without a leash in some situations, but this requires good obedience from him and careful supervision from you. Here are some steps you can follow to safely walk your dog without a leash:

1. **Make sure he is well-trained and obedient.** It is necessary that he responds quickly and effectively to your basic commands, such as "sit,"lie down," and "come."
2. **Choose a safe place to walk your dog off-leash**. Dog parks and dog playgrounds are ideal places where dogs can be off-leash while being supervised.
3. **Maintain a safe distance from other people and animals**. If you encounter other people or animals during the walk, make sure he stays at a reasonable distance and does not approach them without your permission.
4. **Be attentive and ready to intervene if necessary.** Even though he is well-trained, it's important to remain vigilant and regularly remind him of the basic rules. If he starts to wander too far or exhibit undesirable behaviors, call him back and bring him closer to you.

You must comply with the laws and regulations in your area regarding off-leash dogs. If you have any doubts about where your dog can be off-leash, don't hesitate to inquire with your local authorities or a dog trainer.

Learning to stay home alone.

It is important to properly prepare your dog to be alone at home in order to prevent destructive or anxious behaviors that can occur when the dog feels abandoned or stressed. Here are some steps you can follow to teach your dog to stay alone at home:

1. Start with short separation periods. Leave him alone for short periods, then return to reward him with treats and affection. Gradually increase the duration of separation periods.

2. Provide him with toys and chew bones to keep him occupied while you are away. This will help him pass the time and alleviate anxiety.
3. Leave a radio or television on to provide him with company during your absence.
4. Don't make a dramatic departure. Don't give him the impression that you're leaving forever every time you leave the house.
5. Ignore his anxious or destructive behaviors. Don't reward him with attention when he behaves this way, as it could reinforce these undesirable behaviors.

It is advisable to take the necessary time for him to get used to being alone at home and not leave him alone for too long before he is ready.

If he refuses?

If he refuses to stay alone at home or if you notice signs of anxiety or sadness when you leave him alone, here are some tips you can follow:

- Make sure to prepare your dog well to be alone. Follow the steps mentioned earlier to gradually teach him to stay alone, and reward him every time he remains calm and peaceful on his own.
- If he has trouble being alone, you can try to distract him with toys and chew bones to keep him busy while you're away. You can also leave the radio or television on to keep him company.
- If he exhibits destructive or anxious behaviors when alone, it is recommended not to reward him with attention when he behaves this way. This could reinforce these undesirable behaviors.
- Try leaving him an object with your scent to reassure him. It can be a shirt or an old sweater that you have recently worn.
- If he struggles to stay alone and tends to bark or whine when left alone, try teaching him to stay calm on command. You can do this by rewarding him every time he remains calm when you are away.
- If he has serious separation anxiety issues, it may be helpful to consult a veterinarian or a dog behaviorist. These professionals can help you understand why he struggles to stay alone and provide guidance on how to make him feel more secure when he is alone.

It is advisable to take the necessary time for him to get used to being alone at home and not leave him alone for too long before he is ready.

Learning Not to Jump on People

Here are some tips that can help you teach your dog not to jump on people:

- Teach your dog basic commands like "sit,"down," and "stay," which will help him better manage social situations and calm down when in the presence of people.
- Use positive reinforcement to strengthen your dog's desirable behaviors and show him that he can receive rewards when he behaves appropriately.
- If he jumps on people when he's excited, use a firm and immediate "no" to show him that this behavior is not acceptable.
- Ensure he gets enough exercise and entertainment to prevent boredom and restlessness.
- If he jumps on people when he's stressed or anxious, be patient and understanding, and work with a professional to develop stress management strategies tailored to his needs.

- If he jumps on people regularly, make sure to provide him with appropriate alternatives to express his excitement, such as playing with a toy or chasing a ball.
- Finally, remember that dogs are social animals and need physical contact and affection. Make sure to give him plenty of pets and cuddles to fulfill his emotional needs while teaching him not to jump on people.

In summary, teaching your dog not to jump on people may take time and patience, but by following these tips, you can help him understand and manage this behavior appropriately.

Learning not to eat everything lying around.

It's natural for him to try to eat everything lying around because he was bred to hunt and find food. However, it's necessary to teach him not to eat everything lying around, as it can be dangerous for his health and may lead to undesirable behaviors such as food guarding or aggression towards people who are eating. Here are some steps you can follow to teach your dog not to eat everything lying around:

- Don't leave food accessible to your dog. By not leaving food accessible, he won't have the opportunity to find and eat it. Store food in sealed containers and keep trash in a place he can't access.
- Teach him a "leave it" or "no" command. Use the "leave it" or "no" command to ask him to drop an object he has in his mouth. Reward him each time he obeys this command.
- Pay attention to your own eating habits. Don't give him food while you're eating, and don't feed him at the table. If you never give him food while you're at the table, he'll learn that it's not a source of food.
- Be mindful of objects that can be dangerous for your dog. If he tends to eat everything lying around, be vigilant about objects that can be harmful to him, such as toys, shoes, bones, chicken bones, and chemicals. Keep these objects out of his reach or teach him not to touch them.

It may take time for him to stop eating everything lying around, but with patience and diligence, you can teach him this good habit.

If he refuses to obey?

If he refuses to drop an object he has in his mouth, here are some steps you can follow:
- **Don't panic.** If you panic, your dog may become anxious or aggressive. Stay calm and try to restore calmness.
- **Use a firm "leave it" or "no" command.** Use a firm and clear tone to ask him to drop the object. Repeat the command until he obeys.
- **Exchange the object for a treat.** If he won't let go of the object, try offering him a treat in exchange. Place the treat in front of his nose and wait for him to release the object so you can take it.
- **Use gloved hands or tweezers.** If he won't release the object and you can't exchange it for a treat, you can use gloved hands or tweezers to remove the object from his mouth. Be careful not to get bitten or harm your dog.

You should not let your dog eat anything and everything, as it can be dangerous for his health. If he refuses to release an object, stay calm and try to find a peaceful solution. If you're having difficulty, don't hesitate to seek help from a professional.

Learning not to beg at the table.

It's normal for him to try to beg for food while you're at the table because he has learned that it's a potential source of food, and it can be difficult to resist his pleading eyes. However, it's necessary to teach him not to beg while you eat, as it can be impolite and may even lead to undesirable behaviors such as food guarding or aggression towards people who are eating. Here are some steps you can follow to teach your dog not to beg at the table:

1. Ignore begging behaviors. Do not give your dog any food while you eat, even if he appears to be begging. If you respond to his requests, you are teaching him that it works, and he will continue to do it. Instead, completely ignore him while you eat.
2. Establish a dinner routine. Give him his own portion of food at a predetermined time each day, rather than giving him leftovers while you're at the table. This will show him that food is not available while you eat, and he must wait for his own portion.
3. Teach him a "down" command. Use the "down" command to ask him to lie down next to you while you eat. Reward him each time he obeys this command. This will show him that there is another acceptable way to behave while you eat.
4. Pay attention to your own eating habits. Do not leave food accessible to your dog while you eat, and do not feed him at the table. If you never give him food while you are at the table, he will learn that it is not a source of food.

It may take time for him to stop begging while you are at the table, but with patience and diligence, you can teach him this good habit.

How to Prepare for the Arrival of a Baby?

The arrival of a baby can be a time of significant change for your dog, and he needs to be prepared for this event to ease his transition. Here are a few steps you can take to prepare him for the arrival of a baby:

➢ **Start training your dog to obey new rules and limits.** It's important that he understands the basic rules and obeys your commands quickly and effectively. This will help him better understand what is expected of him when the baby arrives.
➢ **Make sure he's used to being handled and touched.** Babies are often curious and will want to touch and explore your dog. Make sure he's used to being handled and touched gently and appropriately.
➢ **Prepare your dog for baby noises and smells.** You can use recordings of baby noises and dirty diapers to accustom your dog to these stimuli.
➢ **Train your dog to be alone for short periods.** When the baby arrives, you'll have less time to spend with your dog, so it's important that he's accustomed to being alone for short periods.
➢ **Prepare your dog for the arrival of visitors.** When the baby arrives, you'll likely have visitors, and your dog should be used to the presence of other people in your home.

Here are some tips for safely introducing your baby to your dog:
➢ Allow your dog to sniff the baby from a distance and reward him each time he remains calm and obedient.
➢ Never leave your dog alone with the baby, even if he appears calm and obedient.
➢ Teach him not to jump on the baby or put his paws on the baby's face. Use treats or rewards to reinforce these rules.
➢ If he tends to be jealous or possessive, you can teach him to accept the baby by giving him treats whenever he's near the baby and rewarding him every time he displays calm and obedient behavior.

How to Contribute to Your Dog's Good Behavior?

Here are some tips to contribute to your dog's good behavior when the baby is around:

➤ Ensure your dog gets enough exercise and mental stimulation so that he remains calm and relaxed in the presence of the baby.

➤ Set clear boundaries for your dog and make sure he respects them. Use basic commands to teach him to stay in his place and not disturb the baby.

➤ Reward your dog whenever he displays calm and obedient behavior in the presence of the baby. This will encourage him to repeat this desirable behavior.

➤ If you notice that he is struggling to adapt to the presence of the baby or showing signs of stress or aggression, do not hesitate to consult a veterinarian or a dog behaviorist for assistance.

In summary, it is necessary to prepare your dog for the arrival of the baby by reviewing basic commands, getting him accustomed to the sounds and smells that will surround him when the baby arrives, and teaching him to respect boundaries and not jump on the baby or get too close to him. By following these tips and being attentive to signs of stress or aggression from your dog, you can help ensure a peaceful and safe coexistence between him and your baby. It is crucial to take the time to prepare your dog for the arrival of a baby to facilitate his transition and ensure the safety of everyone.

Finally, it is essential to prioritize the safety of the baby at all times, even if he appears calm and obedient. Never leave your dog alone with the baby and closely monitor him to ensure he does not pose a danger to your baby.

Learning to Get in the Car?

It's important that he knows how to get in the car safely and comfortably, especially if he travels with you often. Here are some steps to follow:

1. **Make sure he's comfortable with the car.** Before getting in the car, let him explore and sniff around the car at his own pace. Give him treats and toys near the car to encourage him to approach it.

2. **Teach your dog to get in the car on command.** Teach him a command such as "get in" or "car" and reward him every time he obeys. You can use a treat to encourage him to get in the car.

3. **Take short car rides.** Once he's comfortable with the idea of getting in the car, start taking short rides to help him get used to the movement of the car. Take frequent breaks so he can relax and stretch his legs.

4. **Increase the duration of car rides gradually.** Once he's comfortable with short car rides, start gradually increasing the duration of these rides. Take frequent breaks and reward him every time he behaves well in the car.

5. **Pay attention to your dog's safety in the car.** Make sure he is securely restrained or in a crate for his safety and the safety of other passengers. Avoid leaving him alone in the car, especially in hot weather, as he can quickly overheat.

If he refuses to obey?

If he refuses to get in the car, here are some steps you can follow:

• **Be patient.** Don't try to force your dog to get in the car if he doesn't want to. It will only increase his fear, and he will be even less inclined to try again.

• **Ensure he feels secure in the car**. Use a transport crate or safety harness to provide a safe and comfortable place for him. Let your dog explore and sniff around the car at his own pace, and offer treats and toys near the car to encourage him to approach.

It may take some time for him to learn to get in the car, but with patience and diligence, he should be able to do so safely. If he struggles to get used to it, be patient and keep working with him until he is comfortable. If you're having difficulty, don't hesitate to seek help from a professional.

Dealing with a Destructive Dog.

A destructive dog is an animal that tends to destroy objects, whether it's furniture, toys, or any other items within its reach. This behavior can be frustrating for owners and can also cause significant material damage.

What exactly is a destructive dog?
A destructive dog is an animal that tends to repeatedly destroy objects. This behavior can manifest in various ways, such as chewing or gnawing on objects, digging or scratching surfaces, or shredding toys or cushions.

How does a dog become destructive?
There are several reasons why a dog can become destructive. Some of these reasons may be related to emotional or behavioral issues, while others may be linked to environmental factors.

- **Stress caused by fear:** A dog that is afraid of certain things, such as loud noises or unfamiliar people, can become destructive. It may try to destroy objects as a way to relieve stress or to attempt to escape from a stressful situation.
- **Lack of activity:** A dog that doesn't receive enough exercise or mental stimulation can become destructive. Dogs need to expend energy and stay mentally engaged, and if they don't receive these stimuli, they can develop undesirable behaviors, such as destroying objects.
- **Hypersensitivity and hyperactivity:** Some dogs are more prone to being destructive due to their temperament. Hypersensitive or hyperactive dogs may struggle to calm down and focus, and they may have a tendency to destroy objects to expend their excess energy.

How to manage a destructive dog?
Dealing with a destructive dog can be challenging, but here are some steps you can take to try to address the issue:
1. **Identify the cause of the destructive behavior:** You need to understand why your dog is behaving this way. Is it bored? Does it need extra exercise? Is it lacking attention? Understanding the cause will help you find an appropriate solution.
2. **Provide your dog with enough exercise and attention:** Ensure that it receives an adequate amount of physical and mental exercise every day. This can help it expend its energy and feel less stressed and frustrated. Additionally, spend time each day playing with your dog and giving it attention.
3. **Redirect their attention:** If they start to destroy something, try to distract them by giving them a toy or offering an alternative activity. This will teach them to focus on something else rather than inappropriate objects.
4. **Try confining them to a room** where there are no objects to destroy or use a crate or barrier to prevent access to those items.
5. **Use positive reinforcement methods:** When they behave well and do not damage objects, reward them with treats and praise. This will teach them to associate desirable behavior with positive rewards.
6. **Try to teach them to stay calmly and obediently alone.** You can do this by leaving them with a treat or toy to keep them occupied while you are away and rewarding them each time they remain calm and obedient.

7. **Never punish your dog for destructive behavior.** This can reinforce the behavior and make it even harder to stop. Instead, use a reward-based positive approach to encourage desired behavior.

8. If they have destructive behavior that appears to be caused by anxiety or stress, it may be helpful to consult a veterinarian or a canine behaviorist for assistance. These professionals can help you understand why your dog has destructive behavior and provide guidance on how to help them feel better.

9. **Protect your valuable items:** If they tend to destroy certain things in particular, keep them out of your pet's reach. This will help prevent future damage.

Dealing with your dog's destructive behavior can be challenging, but by remaining patient and implementing effective strategies, you should be able to address it.

If they refuse to obey?

It is essential not to lose patience or punish your dog severely for their destructive behavior. This could worsen the problem and weaken your relationship with your pet. Instead, stay calm and patient, and try to find positive solutions to help them overcome this undesirable behavior.

How to stop a dog fight?

Dog fights can be frightening and dangerous, especially when they occur in the presence of people. It is, therefore, important to know how to handle a dog fight safely to prevent injuries and defuse the conflict.

Understanding dog conflicts and their causes.

Dog conflicts can have many causes, including:

- **Aggressiveness or dominance:** Some dogs can be aggressive or dominant over other dogs, which can lead to fights.

- **Object possession:** Dogs may fight over the possession of a toy, treat, or chew bone.

- **Territorial defense:** Dogs can be protective of their home, yard, or person and may fight to defend what they perceive as theirs.

- **Frustration or excitement:** Dogs may fight when they are frustrated or excited, for example, when they cannot play with another dog or when they are in the presence of people or animals they do not know.

Can you prevent the fight?

It is often possible to prevent a dog fight by being attentive to warning signs and intervening promptly. Here are some tips to avoid a fight:

☞ Be vigilant when he is in the presence of other dogs. If you notice signs of tension or aggression, remove your dog before it's too late.

☞ If he tends to be aggressive or possessive, make sure to control him using an appropriate leash and collar and teach him basic commands.

☞ Avoid putting your dog in stressful or frustrating situations, such as walks in crowded places or the presence of people or animals he doesn't know.

☞ If he tends to get excited or overprotective, try to calm him down by providing enough exercise and stimulation and teaching him to calm down on command.

Tips to stop the fight:

Unfortunately, it's not always possible to avoid a dog fight. It's necessary to know how to safely stop a dog fight because it can be dangerous for the dogs and the people present. If a fight breaks out despite all your efforts, here are some tips to safely stop it:

1. **Stay calm.** If you panic, you may further excite the dogs and worsen the situation. Try to stay calm and avoid shouting.
2. **Separate the dogs from the fight area.** If possible, separate the dogs from the fight area by physically separating them or bringing them inside or into a secure enclosure. If that's not possible, use a sturdy object (e.g., an umbrella or a broom handle) to separate them without risking injury to yourself. If you can't separate them, create a barrier between them to keep them apart.
3. **Use an object to distract the dogs.** If you have an object within reach, like pepper spray or a whistle, use it to distract the dogs and divert their attention away from the fight.
4. **Use water to cool them down.** If you have a hose or a water bottle nearby, use them to spray the dogs and cool them down. This can help calm them and stop the fight.
5. **Call for help.** If you are alone and unable to stop the fight, call for help immediately.

It is crucial not to jeopardize your own safety while attempting to separate fighting dogs. If you are alone and cannot stop the fight, call for help immediately. If there are children or elderly individuals nearby, ensure they are safe before attempting anything.

What to do if the dogs refuse to stop fighting?
- ☞ Stopping a dog fight can be challenging, especially if the dogs are highly aroused or aggressive. If the dogs refuse to calm down and stop fighting, it may be helpful to make noise or use an object to distract the dogs and attempt to drive them away. If you cannot end the fight and you are in danger, it is important to move away and contact authorities or the police. Do not try to separate the dogs yourself if you do not have the skills or means to do so safely.
- ☞ It is also important to remember that dogs can be unpredictable, and it is always better to take precautions to prevent fights rather than having to try to stop them once they have started.
- ☞ It is crucial not to jeopardize your own safety while attempting to separate fighting dogs. If you are alone and cannot stop the fight, call for help immediately. If there are children or elderly individuals nearby, ensure they are safe before attempting anything.

Understanding Your Dog's Language.

Dogs' body language is an important form of communication and can help us better understand our pet's feelings. By closely observing your dog's postures, ears, mouth, fur, and tail, you can learn a lot about their emotions and intentions. Here are some examples of what your dog's body language can mean:

- **If they tilt their head to the side,** it can mean they are interested and want to be friends. You can respond by speaking to them gently and offering a reward, like a treat or a pat.
- **If they raise their lips to show their teeth,** it can mean they are aggressive and want you to back away. If this behavior is accompanied by a growl, it can be a clear warning not to approach. In this case, you should not approach and respect their personal space.
- **If their ears are perked up,** it can mean they are curious and want to know more about what's going on. You can respond by speaking to them gently and offering a reward if they behave well.
- **If their ears are back or flat,** it can mean they are uncomfortable or fearful. In this case, don't rush them, reassure them by speaking gently, and offer a reward if they behave well.
- **If they have half-closed eyes,** it can mean they feel safe and relaxed. If their eyes are wide open, it can mean they are excited and ready to play or hunt.
- **If they lift one front paw,** it can mean they want to play. It can also mean they want you to play with them immediately. If they start bounding around you or another dog, it can mean they want you to chase them. You can respond by offering a toy or suggesting a playful activity.
- **If they bound around you or another dog,** it can mean they want you to chase them. You can respond by suggesting a physical activity, like a walk or a game of fetch. In this case, it's necessary to show them that you're the pack leader by giving them simple commands and praising them when they follow them correctly. If this behavior is accompanied by a growl and a gently wagging tail, it can mean they're trying to assert their dominance. In this case, it's crucial to stay calm and show them that you're the pack leader by giving them simple commands and praising them when they follow them correctly.
- **If they have erect ears, a raised tail, and raised neck fur,** it can mean they feel confident and want to assert their dominance. If this behavior is accompanied by a growl and a gently wagging tail, it can mean they want you to know who's the leader.
- **If they crouch down, have a low tail, and bark excessively,** it can mean they're trying to assert dominance. If this behavior is accompanied by licking, it can mean they want to show affection and loyalty. In this case, you should show them that you're the pack leader by giving them simple commands and praising them when they follow them correctly. If this behavior is accompanied by licking, it can mean they want to show affection and loyalty. You can respond by offering a reward or giving them a pet.
- **If they roll onto their back,** it can mean they feel vulnerable and trust their owner. In this case, you should reassure them by speaking gently and offering a reward if they behave well..
- **If their tail is wagging freely,** it can mean they're happy and want to be friends. You can respond by offering a reward or giving them a pet.
- **If their tail wags horizontally, slowly, and forcefully,** it can mean they are aggressive and might bite. In this case, do not approach them and respect their personal space.
- **If their tail is low over their hindquarters,** it can mean they are fearful. In this case, do not startle them and reassure them by speaking gently and offering a reward if they behave well.
- **If their tail is low and wagging,** it can mean they are sorry or want to show submission. In this case, it is advisable not to scold them and reassure them by speaking gently and offering a reward if they behave well.

Understanding Dog Licking:

Licking is a normal behavior in dogs, and they do it for various reasons.

1. **Firstly,** licking is a way for dogs to clean themselves and maintain their skin and coat health. Dogs have sweat glands in their skin that produce a liquid that can be licked and helps them cool down. Licking can also help remove parasites and prevent skin infections.
2. **Secondly,** licking is a way for dogs to express their affection and loyalty towards their owners and fellow dogs. Dogs may lick their owners' faces, hands, or feet to show their affection and submission. Licking can also be used as a form of communication between dogs and humans, as a way to seek attention or demonstrate their submission.
3. **Thirdly,** licking can be a territorial marking behavior. Dogs may lick objects or surfaces to mark their territory and communicate with other dogs. For example, a dog may lick walls or furniture to mark its territory or to signal to other dogs that it is the pack leader.

Excessive licking, however, can be a sign of health or behavioral problems. If a dog licks excessively, it is recommended to consult a veterinarian to rule out any underlying health issues, such as skin problems, allergies, parasites, or eating disorders. Excessive licking can also be caused by separation anxiety, which may manifest as excessive licking of the tail, paws, or skin when the dog is left alone.

To manage excessive licking in dogs, it is important to understand the cause of this behavior and implement strategies tailored to their individual needs. This may include changes in their diet, the use of medications or behavioral therapies, or the establishment of care routines to help reduce anxiety. If you are concerned about your dog's well-being or have questions about excessive licking, it is recommended to consult a veterinarian or animal behaviorist for professional advice. Keeping a journal of your dog's behavior, noting the frequency and duration of excessive licking, as well as the circumstances in which it occurs, can be helpful in identifying triggers and implementing appropriate management strategies.

It is also important to ensure that he receives a balanced and quality diet, as well as access to clean and fresh water. If he has skin or coat problems, it is recommended to brush him regularly and provide quality care to maintain his skin and coat in good health. It can be helpful to establish care routines to reduce separation anxiety and prevent excessive licking when you are away. This may include chew toys to entertain your dog, music or television to keep him company, or positive reinforcement exercises to help him relax and calm down.

Why Does He Dig in the Ground?

Dogs dig in the ground for various reasons.

1. **Firstly,** digging can be an instinctive behavior for dogs, especially those that have been bred for hunting and chasing prey. Dogs may dig to uncover buried prey or to create hiding spots for future hunts.
2. **Secondly,** digging can be a territorial marking behavior for dogs. By digging, dogs can mark their territory and communicate with other dogs. Dogs may also dig to mark their territory by depositing urine or leaving scent traces in the soil.
3. **Thirdly,** digging can be a behavior of distraction or energy expenditure for dogs that are left alone for long periods or do not receive enough exercise. Understimulated or bored dogs may dig to pass the time or to keep themselves occupied.

Finally, digging can be a behavior driven by a search for comfort or coolness for dogs. Dogs may dig to find a cool and shaded spot to rest or to dig a hole to lie in when it's hot.

Understanding the reasons why your dog digs is essential in order to implement appropriate management strategies. If your dog digs out of hunting instinct, it can be helpful to provide chew toys and treats to help channel their energy and satisfy their chewing needs. If they dig to mark their territory, it can be useful to teach them basic commands like "sit" and "lie down" to establish yourself as the pack leader and teach them to calm down.

If they dig out of boredom or under-stimulation, it's important to provide them with enough exercise and entertainment. This can include daily walks, games, and positive reinforcement exercises to help them expend energy and relax. You can also try offering them chew toys and treats to keep them occupied when you're not around.

Lastly, if they dig to find a cool and shaded spot, it's important to ensure they have access to a cool and shaded area in your yard or home. You can also try providing them with a kennel or shelter to allow them to rest in the shade and protect them from the elements.

In summary, dogs dig in the ground for various reasons, including hunting instinct, territorial marking, boredom or under-stimulation, and seeking comfort or coolness. Understanding why your dog digs and implementing management strategies tailored to their individual needs is necessary to manage this behavior appropriately.

Understanding Why He Steals Objects.

There are several reasons why a dog may steal objects.

1. **First**, object stealing can be an instinctive behavior for dogs, especially those selected for hunting and chasing prey. Dogs may steal objects to chew on them, hide them, or to play games like "fetch" and "retrieve."

2. **Secondly,** object stealing can be a behavior of distraction or energy expenditure for dogs that are left alone for extended periods or do not receive enough exercise. Dogs that are bored may steal objects to pass the time or to entertain themselves.

3. **Thirdly,** object stealing can be a behavior related to food-seeking or reward for dogs that are hungry or heavily rewarded when they bring objects. If regularly rewarded when bringing objects, they may be tempted to steal objects to obtain a reward.

Finally, object stealing can be an anxious or stressed behavior for dogs that are anxious or have behavioral problems. If anxious or stressed, they may steal objects in an attempt to calm themselves or distract from their stress.

Understanding the reasons why your dog steals objects is essential to implement appropriate management strategies.

1. **If he steals objects out of hunting instinct,** it can be helpful to provide him with chew toys and treats to help him channel his energy and satisfy his chewing needs.

2. **If he steals objects due to boredom or under-stimulation,** it is recommended to provide him with plenty of exercise and entertainment. This can include daily walks, games, and positive reinforcement exercises to help him expend energy and relax. You can also try offering him chew toys and treats to keep him occupied when you're away.

3. **If he steals objects to obtain a reward,** it is important not to reward him when he brings stolen items and to teach him to obey a "drop" or "exchange" command. You can also try offering alternative rewards, such as treats or toys, to encourage him to only steal those objects.

4. **Your dog steals objects when you are away from home:** If he tends to steal objects when you are absent, he may be suffering from separation anxiety. In this case, it can be helpful to implement positive reinforcement techniques to encourage desirable behaviors when you are not at home (e.g., not stealing objects). You can also establish crisis management protocols to help him cope with his anxiety when you are away (e.g., offering him a toy for distraction).

5. **Your dog steals objects when there are guests at home:** If he tends to steal objects when there are guests at home, he may be fearful or stressed by these new people. In this case, it can be helpful to implement positive reinforcement techniques to encourage desirable behaviors (e.g., not stealing objects) when there are guests at home. You can also establish crisis management protocols to help him cope with his stress or fear (e.g., offering him a quiet and secure place where he can retreat if needed).

6. **Your dog steals objects when there are loud noises or stressful situations:** If he tends to steal objects when there are loud noises or stressful situations, he may be stressed or anxious in these situations. In this case, it can be helpful to implement positive reinforcement techniques to encourage desirable behaviors (e.g., not stealing objects) when there are loud noises or stressful situations. You can also establish crisis management protocols to help him cope with his stress or anxiety (e.g., offering him a toy or a distraction object when there are loud noises).

In summary, dogs steal objects for various reasons, including hunting instinct, boredom or understimulation, seeking food or reward, and anxiety or stress. It is important to understand the reasons why your dog steals objects and to implement management strategies tailored to his individual needs to help manage this behavior appropriately.

Understanding Your Dog's Jealousy.

Dogs can be jealous for various reasons. First, it should be noted that jealousy is a complex behavior that is not unique to humans. Dogs can experience jealousy when they are faced with a situation where they perceive a threat to their relationship with their owner or their access to a reward or valuable object. Here are some examples of situations that can trigger jealousy in dogs:

- The arrival of a new family member, such as a new baby or a new four-legged companion, who receives a lot of attention and rewards from the owner.
- The arrival of a guest or friend who receives a lot of attention and rewards from the owner.
- Sharing the owner's attention and rewards with other pets or other family members.
- Losing access to the dog's preferred objects or activities due to the presence or owner's interest in other things.

How to Identify Their Jealousy?
It should be noted that jealousy is not always easy to identify in dogs, as they cannot express their emotions in the same way as humans. However, here are some signs that may indicate jealousy:

- He shows restlessness or excitement when you are with other people or animals.

- He tries to come between you and other people or animals, or he tries to get your attention by barking or jumping on you.
- He displays aggression or hostility towards other people or animals who receive attention or rewards from you.
- He shows signs of sadness or distress when you are with other people or animals, and he does not have access to your attention or rewards.

How to manage his jealousy?

It is necessary to manage your dog's jealousy appropriately to maintain a healthy and balanced relationship with them. Here are some strategies that can help you manage their jealousy:

- Provide them with enough exercise and entertainment to prevent them from getting bored or feeling neglected.
- Teach them basic commands like "sit,"lie down," and "stay" to show them who is the pack leader and to teach them to calm down.
- Use positive reinforcement to strengthen their desirable behaviors and show them that they can receive rewards when they behave appropriately.
- Ignore undesirable behaviors like restlessness or aggression, and do not reward them when they display jealousy. Instead, reward them when they behave calmly and kindly towards other people or animals.
- Exercise patience and kindness when managing your dog's jealousy. Remember that jealousy is a complex behavior that requires time and perseverance to be appropriately handled.

Jealousy can be a challenging behavior to deal with, but it is possible to work with your dog to help them better understand and manage their emotions. Here are some additional tips that can help you manage their jealousy:

- Offer them plenty of quality time with you, especially when you are with other people or animals. This can help strengthen your relationship with your dog and show them that you are always there for them.
- Avoid over-rewarding your dog when you are with other people or animals. This can reinforce their jealous behavior and make them believe they need to be aggressive or anxious to get your attention.
- Encourage your dog to play with other dogs or interact with other people or animals in a positive way. This can help them develop better social skills and feel less jealous.
- Establish clear routines and rules for your dog so that they know what is expected of them. This can help them feel more secure and less prone to jealousy.

Jealousy can be a normal and healthy behavior for a dog, but excessive jealousy or jealous aggression can be a sign of more serious behavioral issues.

In summary, jealousy is a complex behavior that can be challenging to manage, but it is possible to work with your dog to help them better understand and control their emotions. By using positive reinforcement techniques, offering them plenty of quality time with you, and establishing clear routines and rules, you can help them feel less jealous and develop better social skills.

Understanding Your Dog's Growling

Dogs growl for various reasons. Growling can be a normal and healthy behavior for a dog as a way for them to communicate their emotions or needs. However, it's essential to consider the context in which your dog is growling and monitor their other behaviors to determine if their growling is a sign of more severe behavioral issues.

Here are some reasons why your dog might growl:
- They are trying to communicate that they are in distress or need something. For example, they might growl when they are hungry, thirsty, cold, or when they need to go outside.
- They are trying to assert dominance or defend their territory. Dogs may growl when they feel threatened or want to establish themselves as the pack leader.
- They are trying to communicate that they are angry or frustrated. Dogs may growl when faced with a situation they dislike, such as being forced to do something they don't want to do.

What to do in this case:
Here are some examples of strategies you can implement to manage your dog's growling:
- **Identify the cause of your dog's growling:** To help your dog overcome their growling behaviors, it's crucial to understand what triggers this reaction. This can be challenging, but you can start by keeping a journal of your dog, noting each time they growl and the circumstances surrounding this behavior. This will help you identify potential triggers and implement strategies to manage them.
- **Use positive reinforcement techniques to encourage desirable behaviors**: Positive reinforcement involves rewarding your dog when they exhibit desirable behaviors. For example, if they stop growling when you speak to them, you can reward them with a treat or a favorite toy. This strategy can help them associate positive behaviors with pleasant rewards and thus abandon undesirable behaviors.
- **Use distraction techniques to redirect their attention:** Distraction techniques can be very helpful in helping them overcome anxious or stressful behaviors. For example, if they growl when there are guests at home, you can offer them a toy or a chew bone to distract and divert them from undesirable behaviors.
- **Implement crisis management protocols:** If they continue to growl excessively or destructively, it can be helpful to implement crisis management protocols to respond effectively during a crisis. For example, you can establish "pause" signals for them to stop and calm down or use distraction techniques to divert their attention from stressful situations.
- **Provide a quiet and secure place for them to retreat:** If they are anxious or stressed in certain situations, it can be helpful to provide them with a quiet and secure place where they can retreat if needed. For example, you can give them access to a room or a safety crate where they can withdraw and calm down. You can also offer them toys or chew bones to distract them and help them relax.

You should monitor the context in which your dog growls and observe their other behaviors to determine if there are reasons to be concerned. This can help you identify the causes of these behaviors and implement management strategies tailored to their needs.

Preventing Fights in My Dog.

There are several strategies you can implement to prevent fights in your dog:
- Ensure that they receive enough exercise and entertainment to prevent boredom or restlessness.

- Teach them basic commands like "sit,"lie down," and "stay" to establish leadership and teach them to calm down.
- Use positive reinforcement to reinforce your dog's desirable behaviors and show them that they can receive rewards when behaving appropriately.
- Avoid putting them in stressful or confrontational situations, such as leaving them alone with unfamiliar dogs or exposing them to food or toys that could lead to fights.
- If your dog tends to be aggressive towards other dogs, avoid leaving them alone with others and make sure you always have control of the situation by using a leash and harness.
- If you notice signs of stress or aggression in the presence of other dogs, remove them from the situation immediately and set up a physical barrier to separate them.

You must identify the causes of their aggression and implement management strategies tailored to their individual needs.

What to do about dog aggression?

Here's how I could behave when confronted with a dog that curls its lips to show its teeth:

- First and foremost, I would ensure to remain calm and not display my fear or anxiety in front of the dog. If the dog senses that I am anxious or afraid, it could make them even more aggressive.
- I would take the time to observe the dog and make sure I understand what's going on. Does the dog show its teeth only in specific situations (e.g., when there's food or when there are other dogs present)? Is the dog consistently displaying this behavior, or is it an isolated incident? Is the dog trying to protect its territory, or is it reacting instinctively to a perceived threat?
- Based on what I observe, I would determine the best approach to handle the dog's aggressive behavior. If the dog consistently shows its teeth or is aggressive towards humans or other animals, I may need to seek professional assistance. If the dog only shows its teeth in specific situations, I could work on those specific situations to teach the dog to react appropriately. I must teach the dog basic commands (such as "sit,"lie down,"heel") to establish myself as the pack leader and help the dog learn to calm down.
- You would also teach positive reinforcement techniques to reinforce your dog's desirable behaviors and show that they can receive rewards when behaving appropriately. For example, if he barks aggressively when there are other dogs in the street, you might recommend rewarding him when he stays calm and not rewarding him when he barks.
- If I find myself in a situation where I have to provide veterinary care or basic care to the dog in question, I would make sure to take all necessary precautions to protect myself. This could include using protective gear (such as gloves or safety goggles) or setting up physical barriers (such as a crate or a gate) to shield myself from bites. If I need to handle the dog, I would do so gently and gradually and praise it each time it behaves well. If the dog continues to show signs of aggression despite my efforts to calm it, I might consult a veterinarian to assess whether there are any health issues underlying its aggressive behavior.
- If it displays aggression towards humans, you would advise caution and not approach the dog when it's in an excited state. If it shows signs of aggression towards other dogs, I would also recommend being cautious and not leaving it alone with other dogs if it has a tendency to be aggressive.
- If the dog shows its teeth aggressively, I would try to show it that I am the pack leader by asserting dominance in a calm and firm manner. This could include techniques such as "head lowering" (tilting the head down and making eye contact with the dog) or "calm dominance" (maintaining eye contact with the dog and showing confidence and control). These techniques are intended to show the dog that you are the pack leader and teach it to respect you.

If you're dealing with his aggressiveness in various situations, here are some steps you can follow:

If he is aggressive because he is afraid:

1. 1.**Identify the source of his fear:** Understanding what is causing your dog's fear can help you better manage the situation and provide adequate support.

2. 2.**Desensitization and conditioning:** This technique involves exposing your dog to frightening stimuli in a controlled manner and rewarding him for good behavior. This can help reduce his fear and reinforce positive behavior.

3. 3.**Use rewards:** Encourage your dog by rewarding him when he reacts calmly and confidently to stressful situations. This can help him associate these situations with something positive.

4. 4.**Create a safe environment:** Ensure that he has a secure and comfortable place to retreat to when he feels stressed or frightened.

If he is aggressive to protect his territory or family:

1. **Identify triggers:** Determine what triggers his aggression. Is it when he sees strangers, other animals or when he feels threatened in some way? Knowing the triggers will help you better prevent or manage your dog's aggression.

2. **Avoid stressful situations:** If possible, avoid putting your dog in situations that stress him or may trigger his aggression. For example, if he's aggressive towards other animals, avoid walking him in areas where there are lots of other animals.

3. **Reinforce positive behavior:** Use positive reinforcement to encourage him to adopt calm, relaxed behaviors when confronted by strangers or other animals. For example, give him a reward when he remains calm and seated when approached by a stranger.

4. **Show firm leadership:** Make sure he respects and obeys you. Be the leader of your family and show him that you're in charge and that you care for him. This will help him feel secure and less inclined to be aggressive.

5. **Use control commands:** Teach him control commands like "sit" and "down" that he can use to calm himself when faced with stressful situations. Use these commands regularly and reward him when he executes them correctly.

6. .**Train your dog:** Exercise and train him regularly to keep him fit and calm. Physical exercise can help reduce his aggression by expelling his energy and keeping him in a positive state of mind.

If he is aggressive during play:

- ·**Monitor your dog during play:** Watch your dog closely during play to spot signs of stress or excitement. If he shows signs of stress or aggression, immediately interrupt the game and calm him down before allowing him to resume.

- ·**Teach him appropriate play behaviors:** Use positive reinforcement to encourage him to exhibit appropriate play behaviors, such as biting gently and releasing on command.

- ·**Take regular breaks:** Take regular breaks during play so he can calm down and catch his breath. This will help him better manage his excitement and avoid becoming aggressive.

- ·**Use appropriate play toys**: Use play toys that cannot be easily damaged or broken and are not dangerous for him. This will help prevent injuries and reduce aggression during play.

- ·**Exercise and train your dog regularly**: Regular physical exercise can help drain your dog's energy and keep him in a calm and relaxed state of mind.

If he becomes aggressive under the influence of his hunting instinct:

1. **FExercise and train your dog regularly:** Regular physical exercise can help drain his energy and keep him in a calm and relaxed state of mind.
2. **2.Teach him control commands:** Use positive reinforcement to teach your dog control commands like "sit" and "down" that he can use to calm himself when confronted with other animals.
3. **3.Show firm leadership:** Ensure that he respects and obeys you. Be the leader of your family and show him that you are in charge and taking care of him. This will help him feel secure and less prone to aggression.
4. **4.Use distraction toys:** If he becomes aggressive when he sees other animals, use distraction toys to divert his attention. For example, give him a chew toy or a bone to chew on when he is confronted with other animals to help him ignore them.

Seek professional help:

If you have difficulty managing your dog's aggression due to frustration, don't hesitate to seek help from an animal behaviorist or professional trainer. They can help you understand the causes of his frustration and implement strategies to manage it appropriately. By working with a professional dog trainer and implementing strategies tailored to your dog and your situation, you should be able to better manage your dog's aggression and create a positive and harmonious relationship with him.

Activities and Leisure:

Dogs are very active and intelligent animals that require a lot of exercise and mental stimulation to stay happy and healthy. Here are some activities and leisure activities that you can enjoy with your dog:

- **Take regular walks.**

Dogs need a lot of exercise and physical activity. Make sure to walk your dog every day to allow them to expend energy and explore new places. You can also vary the walking routes to make the walks more interesting for them.

- **Walking:** walking is a simple but very beneficial activity for your dog. In addition to providing exercise and physical activity, walking allows them to discover new places and strengthen their bond with you.
- **Benefit:** Walking can help them stay fit and expend their energy. It can also strengthen your bond with them and allow them to discover new places.
- **How to practice it?** For walking, you can simply take your dog with you during your daily walk. You can also vary the walking routes to make the walks more interesting for them.

- **Play with him.**

Dogs love to play, and this can be an excellent way to strengthen your bond with your dog. You can play games like fetch, frisbee, or recall with them to provide exercise and mental stimulation. You can also provide them with chew toys and scratch toys to keep them busy when they are alone at home.

- **Treasure Hunt:** Treasure hunt is an entertaining game that involves hiding treats or toys for your dog to find. This activity can be very entertaining for your dog and provide mental stimulation.
- **Benefit:** Treasure hunt can help develop their reasoning ability and keep them entertained when they are alone at home.
- **How to practice:** You can hide treats or toys in your house or garden for them to find. You can also purchase or make treasure hunt toys for them.

- **Engage in Reinforcement Training.** Reinforcement training is an excellent way to provide mental stimulation and strengthen your bond with your dog. You can use treats to reinforce desired behaviors and teach new tricks.
- **Participate in Sports with Him.** If he enjoys exercise and you are athletic, you can try engaging in sports with him. For example, you can go running or biking with him or even try canine sports like agility or obedience.

Here are some activities and pastimes that can be adapted for your dog:

These are fun athletic activities for you and your dog that can help:

1. Strengthen your bond with your pet.
2. Improve your dog's physical fitness.
3. Enhance his coordination and improve his ability to follow your commands.
4. Mentally stimulate your dog by providing new experiences and allowing him to express himself.

Agility

Agility is a high-intensity sport that involves guiding your dog through an obstacle course.

Here is a detailed example of steps to teach your puppy agility:

- Find a local agility club or trainer who can guide you and provide advice on how to get started.

- Ensure that your puppy is in good physical condition and has received all necessary vaccinations before starting agility training. This activity can be physically demanding, so it's important that your puppy is fit and safe.

- Start with basic exercises to help develop your puppy's movement and coordination skills. You can use hurdles, tunnels, low bars to jump over, and other small obstacles to help them learn to navigate a course.

- Encourage your puppy to follow your instructions and focus on you using positive reinforcements such as treats or praise. This will help your puppy understand what you expect from them and stay focused during training.

- Increase the difficulty of exercises and courses gradually by adding new obstacles and increasing the exercise speed. This will help your puppy improve their skills and stay motivated.

- Use positive reinforcement techniques to encourage desired behavior and to correct your puppy's mistakes in a positive manner. Avoid shouting or punishing your puppy when they make mistakes as it may discourage or stress them.

- If you encounter difficulties or have questions about working with your puppy in agility, don't hesitate to seek help from a certified trainer or a professional dog educator. They can provide you with specific advice and techniques to effectively and enjoyably teach your puppy agility.

It's important not to forget that every dog is different, and the pace at which they learn depends on their own abilities and personality. Be patient and encourage your dog with rewards and positive reinforcement to help them progress in their advanced training.

Treibball.

Treibball is a sport where you send your dog to push balls of different sizes into a goal.
To practice Treibball, here are some steps to follow:
- Find a local Treibball club or trainer who can guide you and provide advice on how to get started.
- Start with basic exercises like pushing a ball with their nose or paw.
- Gradually increase the difficulty of the exercises by adding more balls or arranging them in different ways.
- Train regularly with your dog to improve their skills and fitness.

Cani-cross

Cani-cross is a sport where you run with your dog on a leash attached to your belt.
To practice cani-cross, here are some steps to follow:
- Find a local cani-cross club or trainer who can guide you and provide advice on getting started.
- Ensure that your dog is in good physical condition before starting to run with them.
- Start with short distances and gradually increase the distance and duration of your cani-cross sessions.
- Wear a cani-cross belt to support your dog and prevent any risk of injury.
- Train regularly with your dog to improve their skills and fitness.

Rally Obedience

Rally obedience is a sport where you and your dog navigate through an obedience course following signs indicating commands to perform.

To practice rally obedience, here are some steps to follow:

- Find a local rally obedience club or trainer who can guide you and provide advice on getting started.
- Ensure that your dog has mastered basic obedience commands before moving on to rally obedience.
- Start with beginner-level courses and gradually increase the difficulty of exercises by adding distractions and working at longer distances.
- Train regularly with your dog to improve its skills and reinforce obedience.

Ring

Ring is a competitive sport where you and your dog perform a series of commands and obedience exercises in front of a judge.

To practice ring, here are some steps to follow:

1. Find a local ring club or trainer who can guide you and provide advice on how to get started.

YOUSSEFFFF 501YOUSSEFFFF 502

2. Ensure that he masters basic obedience commands before moving on to the ring.
3. Learn the rules of the ring and the judge's scoring criteria.
4. Train regularly with your dog to improve its skills and reinforce obedience.
5. Participate in local ring competitions to gain experience and improve your skills.

Very important:

If he refuses to do any of the activities mentioned above, it is advisable not to force him or put him under pressure. Try to find ways to make training fun and encouraging for your dog by using rewards and taking regular breaks for him to rest. If he continues to refuse to do this activity, he may simply not be interested in this type of activity, and it is necessary to respect his needs and find other ways to spend time together.

Learning Tricks.

Dog tricks are an excellent way to keep your dog mentally and physically sharp. All dog owners should ensure that their pets have a healthy repertoire of tricks they can perform, not just to show off but for their well-being.

You can teach your dog tricks using positive reinforcement techniques and by being patient and persistent. Here are some steps to follow to teach your dog tricks:

1. Choose a trick to teach your dog. Select a trick that suits your dog based on their age, size, and abilities.
2. Start by breaking down the trick into simple steps. For example, if you want to teach him to sit, begin by having him raise his rear paw to sit.
3. Reward your dog every time he successfully completes a step of the trick. Use treats or praise to congratulate him and motivate him to learn.
4. Repeat each step of the trick several times until he masters it.
5. Once he has mastered each step of the trick, start chaining them together to perform the complete trick.

6. Continue to reward your dog every time he successfully performs the trick, but gradually reduce the frequency of rewards over time to encourage him to maintain his performance.

What to Do If He Refuses to Obey?

If he refuses to perform the trick you asked for, there are several things you can try:
1. **Make sure he understands what you expect from him.** If you have trouble getting him to understand what you want from him, he may become discouraged quickly.
2. **Check if he is not stressed or anxious.** If he is anxious or stressed, it can be difficult for him to focus on the exercise and relax.
3. **Be patient and do not force your dog to do the trick if he is not interested.** If he doesn't like kisses, he may prefer other positive reinforcement activities or mental stimulation.
4. **Keep training sessions short and fun** to maintain your dog's interest and encourage learning. Remember to be patient and persistent, as learning a trick can take time and repetition.

It's also important to remember never to force your dog to give kisses if he doesn't want to, and to respect his boundaries. If he doesn't like kisses, he may prefer other positive reinforcement activities or mental stimulation.

Learning to Shake Hands.

"Hello" is a simple but useful command that you can teach your dog. It involves standing on their hind legs and extending their front paw to greet. Here's how you can teach them to say "hello":
- Choose a quiet and distraction-free place to start training your dog.
- Start by encouraging them to stand on their hind legs by holding a treat in front of their nose and asking them to "say hello." Reward them each time they stand on their hind legs.
- Once they are comfortable with the idea of standing on their hind legs, start showing them how to extend their front paw by placing a treat under their paw and asking them to shake hands while saying "hello."
- Reward him each time he performs a "hello" correctly and repeat the exercise several times until he understands what you expect from him.
- Once he understands the "hello" command, you can start asking him to perform it without a treat and teach him a specific command word, such as "hello" or "hi."

Learning to kiss.

The "kiss" is a fun and affectionate trick you can teach your dog. It involves touching your face with their paw or nose on command. Here's how you can teach them to give kisses:

1. Choose a quiet and distraction-free place to start training your dog.
2. Start by encouraging them to touch your face with their paw by holding a treat near your face and asking for a "kiss." Reward them each time they touch your face with their paw.
3. Once they are comfortable with the idea of touching your face with their paw, start showing them how to touch your face with their nose by holding a treat near your face and asking for a "kiss."
4. Reward them each time they perform a correct kiss and repeat the exercise several times until they understand what you expect from them.

5. Once they understand the "kiss" command, you can start asking them to do it without a treat and teach them a specific command word, such as "kiss" or "give a kiss."

Learning to sing.

It is possible to teach your dog to bark on command, which can be fun for both you and your dog. However, it's important to remember that dogs are not humans and they can't really sing like we do. Here's how you can teach your dog to bark on command:
1. Choose a command that you will use every time you want him to bark, such as "speak" or "bark."
2. Encourage your dog to bark by making noise or waving a toy in front of him. When he barks, reward him and repeat this exercise several times until he understands what you expect from him.
3. Once he understands how to bark on command, start asking him to bark when he is calm, giving him a reward each time he barks on command.
4. Repeat this exercise several times until he understands how to bark on command, even when he is calm.

Learning to dance.

It is possible to teach your dog to perform certain movements on command, such as lifting a paw or spinning around. This can be fun for both you and your dog, but it's important to remember that dogs are not humans and they can't really dance like we do. Here's how you can teach your dog to perform certain movements on command:

1. Repeat this exercise several times until he understands how to perform the movement on command, even when he is calm.

Learning to smile

You can make it appear like your dog is smiling by teaching him to open his mouth on command. Here's how you can do it:
1. Choose a command that you will use every time you want him to open his mouth, such as "show teeth" or "lower jaw."
2. Encourage your dog to open his mouth by placing a reward near his mouth or gently pressing on his lower jaw. When he opens his mouth, reward him and repeat this exercise several times until he understands what you expect from him.
3. Once he understands how to open his mouth on command, start asking him to do it when he is calm, rewarding him each time he opens his mouth on command.
4. Repeat this exercise several times until he understands how to open his mouth on command, even when he is calm.

Learning to Back Up

"Backing up" is a useful skill you can teach your dog. It involves getting your dog to move backward on command. Here's how you can do it:
1. Choose a quiet and distraction-free location to start training your dog.

2. Start by encouraging your dog to back up by walking towards him and asking him to "back up." Reward him each time he takes a step backward.
3. Once he's comfortable with the idea of backing up, start showing him how to back up on command by placing a treat behind him and asking him to "back up."
4. Reward your dog each time he successfully backs up and repeat the exercise several times until he understands what you expect from him.
5. Once he understands the command to back up, you can start asking him to do it without a treat and teach him a specific command word, like "back up."

Learning to Roll

"Roll over" is a fun trick you can teach your dog. It involves rolling onto their back on command. Here's how you can teach them to do it:
1. Choose a quiet and distraction-free place to begin training your dog.
2. Start by encouraging your dog to roll onto their back by placing a treat on their back and asking them to "roll over." Reward them each time they roll over.
3. Once they are comfortable with the idea of rolling onto their back, begin showing them how to roll over on command by placing a treat on their back and asking them to "roll over."
4. Reward your dog each time they perform a proper roll and repeat the exercise several times until they understand what you expect from them.
5. Once they understand the roll command, you can start asking them to perform it without a treat and teach them a specific command word, like "roll" or "roll over."

Learning to swim.

It is essential for your dog's safety, especially if they live near water or if you plan to take them on a trip near water. Here are some steps to teach them how to swim:
1. Choose a safe place to teach your dog to swim. A lake or a shallow pool with a flat edge and little current is ideal. Avoid places with a lot of boat traffic or strong currents.
2. Make sure they are comfortable in the water. Start by giving them toys and treats near the water to encourage them to go in. Let them wade in the water and swim, supporting them if needed.
3. Teach your dog to swim using a flotation device or life jacket. If they have trouble staying on the water's surface, a flotation device or life jacket can help them float and move in the water. Put it on your dog and encourage them to swim by praising them and giving treats.
4. Teach them to swim without assistance. Once they seem comfortable in the water and are swimming using a flotation device or life jacket, gradually remove the assistance and encourage them to swim on their own. Reward them each time they swim without assistance.
5. Teach them how to get back to the shore. If they end up in the water and cannot make it back to shore, it is essential that they know how to climb back onto the shore or onto a floating object. Teach them to cling to a raft or buoy and hoist themselves up to get out of the water.

Take your time and adapt the swimming lessons to your dog. If they are afraid of the water or do not seem comfortable, stop the training and try again later. With patience and diligence, they should be able to swim safely.

What if they refuse?

It's normal for him to be afraid of water or refuse to swim, especially if he has never been exposed to water before. If he refuses to swim, here are some steps you can take to help him overcome this fear:

1. Be patient. Don't try to force your dog to swim if he doesn't want to. This will only increase his fear, and he will be even less inclined to try again.
2. Give him time to get used to the water. Let your dog wade and explore the water at his own pace. Encourage him to enter it by giving him treats and praising him every time he puts his paws in.
3. Use a flotation device or life jacket to help him float. If he has trouble staying on the water's surface, a buoy or life jacket can help him float and move in the water. Put it on your dog and encourage him to swim by praising him and giving him treats.
4. Take frequent breaks. If he seems stressed or anxious during training, take a break and let him relax before continuing.
5. It may take time for him to learn to swim, but with patience and diligence, he should be able to overcome his fear of water and swim safely.

Learning to Touch.

Touch is a useful skill you can teach him. It involves touching an object or surface with his paw or nose on command. Here's how you can teach him to touch:

1. Choose a quiet and distraction-free place to begin training your dog.
2. Start by encouraging him to touch an object with his paw by placing a treat in front of the object and asking him to "touch." Reward him each time he touches the object with his paw.
3. Once he is comfortable with the idea of touching an object with his paw, begin to show him how to touch a surface with his nose by placing a treat in front of the surface and asking him to "touch."
4. Reward your dog each time he performs a correct touch and repeat the exercise several times until he understands what you expect from him.
5. Once he understands the "touch" command, you can start asking him to perform it without a treat and teach him a specific command word, such as "touch" or "press."

What if he refuses to obey?

Here are some tips to continue working with your dog on the "touch" command:

1. Vary the surfaces and objects you use to train your dog to keep his interest and reinforce his understanding of the command.
2. Use high-quality treats and toys to positively reinforce your dog each time he performs a correct touch.
3. Conduct short training sessions to avoid overworking your dog and maintain his level of motivation.
4. Be patient and encouraging with him, especially if he struggles to learn the "touch" command.
5. If he has difficulty learning "touch," you can try showing him how to do it by guiding him with your hand or using a laser pointer to help him understand what you expect from him.

In summary, "touch" is a useful skill that you can teach him using treats, toys, and positive reinforcement.

Learning the Bow.

Bowing is a fun and useful trick you can teach him. It involves pausing and lying on his back while showing his belly. Here's how you can teach him to perform the bow:

1. Choose a quiet and distraction-free location to start training your dog.
2. Begin by encouraging him to lie on his back by rolling him over with a treat or gently tapping his belly. Reward him each time he lies on his back.
3. Once he is comfortable with the idea of lying on his back, begin to show him how to lift his front paws by placing a treat under his nose and asking him to "bow."
4. Reward your dog every time he performs a bow correctly and repeat the exercise several times until he understands what you expect from him.
5. Once he understands the bow command, you can start asking him to perform the bow without a treat and teach him a specific command word, such as "bow" or "take a bow."
6. Repeat the exercise several times until he perfectly understands the bow command and performs it on cue.

Teaching to Play Dead

It is possible to teach him to lie on his back and not move when you give him the command "play dead." This can be a fun skill for your dog and for you, but it can also be useful in certain situations, such as when you need to trim his nails or give him an injection. Here's how you can teach him this trick:
1. Start by encouraging him to lie on his back by placing a reward near his back and saying "play dead."
2. When he lies on his back, reward him and repeat this exercise several times until he understands what you expect from him.
3. Once he understands how to lie on his back, start asking him to stay still when he is in this position by giving him a reward every time he remains still.
4. Repeat this exercise several times until he understands how to play dead on command.

Teaching a Sad Face

It is possible to teach him to perform certain movements on command, such as lifting a paw or spinning around. This can be fun for you and your dog, but it's important to remember that dogs are not humans and they can't really make a sad face like we do. However, it is possible to make him look sad by teaching him to lower his head on command. Here's how you can teach him to lower his head on command:

1. Choose a command that you will use every time you want him to lower his head, such as "sad" or "lower your head."
2. Encourage your dog to lower his head by placing a reward near his front paws and using the chosen command. When he lowers his head, reward him and repeat this exercise several times until he understands what you expect from him.
3. When he understands how to lower his head on command, start asking him to do it when he is calm by rewarding him every time he lowers his head on command.
4. Repeat this exercise several times until he understands how to lower his head on command, even when he is calm.

It's important to remain patient and not force your dog to lower his head if he doesn't immediately understand what you expect from him.

Learning to play hide and seek.

Here's how you can teach him to play the hide-and-seek game:
- Start by choosing a safe and suitable place to play hide and seek, such as your home or your garden.
- Demonstrate what you expect from him. Hide behind an object or in a room and call your dog to find you. Reward him with treats or cuddles when he finds you.
- Once he understands the concept of the game, you can increase the difficulty by hiding in more challenging places to find.
- Encourage your dog to use his sense of smell to find your hiding spot by giving him scent clues, such as a treat or a toy that you've handled before hiding.
- Reward your dog every time he finds your hiding spot quickly and effectively. This will encourage him to repeat the desired behavior.

It's important to stay patient and not hide for too long, especially if it's the first time he's playing the hide-and-seek game.

Learning to fetch objects.

Fetching is an important skill for all dogs and can be useful in many situations, such as when you play with them or when you go for a walk on a leash. Here's how you can teach your dog to fetch:
- Choose a fetching object suitable for your dog, such as a ball or a rubber toy. Make sure the object is large enough for him to easily pick up in his mouth and durable enough so that he doesn't destroy it quickly.
- Start by playing with him using this object and encourage him to pick it up in his mouth. When he has the object in his mouth, encourage him to come to you by saying "fetch" or tapping your leg.
- Reward your dog each time he fetches the object by praising him and giving him a treat.
- Repeat this exercise several times until he understands what you expect from him. You can also increase the distance between you and your dog to make the exercise more challenging.
- Once he understands the concept of fetching, you can start teaching him to drop the object on command. To do this, hold a treat in front of him and wait for him to release the fetching object. Reward him immediately when he releases the object and repeat the exercise until he understands the command.

Learning to fetch objects.

Teaching your dog to turn off the light can be a fun and entertaining trick for him, but it's important to remember that the safety of your dog and your home should be your top priority. Here's how you can teach him to turn off the light:

- Choose a quiet and distraction-free place to begin training your dog.
- Start by encouraging him to touch the light switch with his paw by placing a treat near the switch and asking him to "turn it off." Reward him every time he touches the switch with his paw.
- Once he's comfortable with the idea of touching the switch, begin showing him how to turn off the light by placing a treat near the switch and asking him to "turn it off."
- Reward your dog every time he successfully follows this command, and repeat the exercise several times until he understands what you expect from him.

- Once he understands the command to turn off the light, you can start asking him to do it without a treat and teach him a specific command word like "turn off" or "switch off the light."

Conclusion:

Your journey with the Border Collie is an epic of connection and understanding, a story that unfolds every day between you and your loyal companion. This comprehensive book on Border Collie training has guided you through the smallest details to educate, train, communicate with your dog, and understand his unique language.

Throughout the pages, we've explored the fascinating origin of this exceptional breed, the physical and behavioral aspects that make him an outstanding companion, and practical advice for welcoming your puppy, taking care of his health at every stage of his life, and making him happy through training and activities.

Always remember that your Border Collie is much more than just a pet; he is your loyal friend, your partner, your source of priceless joy. By learning to decode his language, respond to his needs, and live in harmony, you've woven an unbreakable bond.

Now, let this book become a valuable resource for you, a source of reminders and advice when you need it. May every interaction with your Border Collie be an opportunity to strengthen this special bond between you and celebrate the wonderful world of dogs.

The journey you've taken to understand and educate your Border Collie is paved with patience, love, and dedication. With this knowledge and understanding, you hold the key to providing your dog with a fulfilling and healthy life, and you also have the opportunity to live an extraordinary adventure filled with precious moments.

May you and your Border Collie continue to write beautiful pages together, explore new activities, learn from each other, and build a bond that will never stop growing. Your Border Collie is more than just a dog; he is a cherished member of your family, and every moment spent together is a unique adventure.
May your journey with your Border Collie be filled with laughter, companionship, and unforgettable memories. Take care of your loyal companion, cherish every moment, and know that you have everything it takes to give him an exceptional life. Enjoy this extraordinary relationship with your Border Collie, and may this beautiful adventure continue to flourish, day after day.

Made in United States
Troutdale, OR
06/30/2024

20918400R00069